GROWING TO SHOW

how to grow prize-winning african violets

Original text and illustrations by
Pauline Bartholomew

2008 Revision
Barbara Pershing, Editor
AVSA Publications Committee

2008 Edition

COVER PHOTO
'Fresh Air' 2008 New Introduction
Hybridizer, Kent Stork
Photo, Joyce Stork

Contents

Introduction

Pauline Bartholomew, grower of prize-winning show plants, experienced show judge, and creative illustrator wrote and illustrated the first *Growing to Show* in 1985. It has been reprinted several times since then with only minor additions. The African Violet Society of America, Inc., is grateful for her gift, in 2003, of all rights to the book

Much of the information from the original text has not changed significantly, but new research and new products have added greatly to growers' knowledge and resources. Computers and the Internet have made new information far more accessible; AVSA has extended its influence and its help to growers all over the world through the AVSA website. New research and scientific DNA testing have added to our knowledge of the *Saintpaulia* species and a new taxonomy has been introduced.

The Publications Committee was given the responsibility to retain the wisdom in this valuable book and bring it up to date. We have kept a great deal of Pauline's writing and most of her illustrations from the first editions. We have added information on plant types, blossom and foliage types, watering methods, pH testing, pesticides, and light options. The information on growing and showing miniatures and semiminiatures has been expanded and a section on Saintpaulia species has been added. We have added information on the African Violet Society of America, Inc., it's publications, and AVSA judging standards.

Although the title of this book is *Growing to Show*, it has been widely recommended as the best available resource for anyone growing African violets, whether for show or pleasure. We have endeavored to add information to this resource for beginning growers as well as for experienced growers who have grown and shown award-winning African violets for many years.

Publications committee members and other AVSA members who have contributed their time and knowledge to this revision include: Barbara Pershing, Barbara Werness, Carolee Carter, Randy Deutsch, Susan Anderson, Catherine Thompson, Martha Menard, Gail Podany, and Marjorie Bullard.

The following individuals have contributed their expertise to this revision: Paul Sorano for sharing his knowledge of current pesticides; Ralph Robinson for his thoughts on lighting; Kathi Lahti and Anne Nicholas for adding to the information on miniatures and semiminiatures; Richard Nicholas for sharing his expertise on growing and showing standards; Dr. Jeff Smith for being there to answer e-mails on any number of topics including the new species taxonomy; Joe Bruns, Chairman of AVSA Registration Committee for up-to-date information on registration numbers and *First Class* data; Bill Foster, Chairman of Shows and Judges Committee; and Joyce Stork, President, and Ron Davidson, 1st Vice President of AVSA for their support and encouragement throughout the revision process.

Photo credits go to Tom Glembocki, photographer, AVSA Library Committee, and to Janet McDowell for the cover and photo page designs.

Barbara Pershing, Editor
AVSA Publications Committee Chairman

1985-2001 Editions

The following introduction to the earlier editions of *Growing to Show*, written by Pauline Bartholomew, explains her purpose for writing this book as well as her philosophy of growing prize-winning African violets:

This manual was written primarily to teach beginners how to grow prize-winning African violets. I hope to help eager newcomers bypass the years of frustration and "growing pains" – not to mention the expensive mistakes – I experienced before winning any top awards.

The manual will also benefit the grower who has advanced to respectable blue ribbon plants but has yet to realize the thrill of winning a top award. Many good growers fall just short of winning a Best in Show award or one of the AVSA Collection Awards. Yet, it takes only the application of a few of the advanced techniques to push a merely good plant into becoming a top award winner.

I occasionally mention a few tips for the casual grower, but for the most part, this manual is for the hobbyist who is dedicated to growing African violets for competitive showing.

The methods explained here are ones I developed after learning about Texas Style potting in 1975. Since then I have won more than my fair share of awards. There are other equally successful ways to grow prizewinning African violets, but I offer none of the alternatives. That is a book for someone else to write.

At first reading, the processes may seem hopelessly complicated. Don't be dismayed. For the first year, refer only to the basics. For instance, fluorescent-light growing is a complex subject, but the summary tells you all you need to know. If the instructions for potting layers and watering confuse you, refer to the summary chart (p. 56). After you have become experienced, the more technical details will be of interest to you.

Refer to the manual each time you work with your plants. Follow the basic procedures step-by-step and soon each process will become second nature to you. The manual then will be needed only as a reference book.

Creating a show plant of ultimate perfection requires a balance of all conditions and processes so don't stray from following the procedures. The time to be innovative is after you have become truly proficient in the methods offered here. And finally, Learn the Language of African violets and show growers.

    Good luck and happy growing,

Pauline Bartholomew

'Mary D' was on the cover of the 1985 through 2001 editions of "Growing to Show". The following was Pauline's 1985 tribute to this plant: "hybridized by the late Max Maas. I purchased the plant at the 1975 AVSA convention in Boston, Massachusetts. Eight times in ten years it has been either first, second, or third Best in Show or one of the AVSA (gold rosette) Collection. It has had a long neck potted down so many times that the only thing left of the original plant is its genetic memory."

Meet Some Award-winning Show Plants

The photos on the following pages were selected from among the many award winning African violets at recent African Violet Society of America, Inc. Convention Shows. The photos were selected from AVSA Library convention photos. Plant descriptions are from the *African Violet Master List of Species and Cultivars (AVML)*. See pages 9 through 12 for descriptions of the many plant, blossom and foliage types found in these descriptions and represented in the photos.

'Rebel's Rose Bud' (#9288–2003), the Best African violet in Show at the 2007 Denver convention, was hybridized by Ruth Bann and exhibited by Richard Nicholas. 'Rebel's Rose Bud' is a double light pink two-tone star with ruffled fuchsia edge. The foliage is variegated dark green and cream, pointed, and quilted with red back. This plant was also the best standard plant in the show.

'Alliance' (#8663–1997) was the Best African violet in the 2006 Minneapolis Show. Hybridized by D. Croteau and exhibited by Catherine Thompson, this plant is described as semidouble medium blue star with white and pink fantasy blossoms and variegated green, cream and pink foliage; this plant was the best standard plant in this show.

'Tropical Heat Wave' (# 8929–2001) was third Best African Violet in the Minneapolis 2006 Show. Hybridizer Kent Stork described this standard plant as having single-semidouble dark coral-rose large frilled star blossoms with dark green, wavy foliage. Catherine Thompson was the exhibitor.

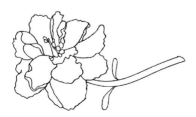

'Buckeye Especially Mine' (#9065–2001) was one of the three plants in the Best Buckeye Collection at the 2007 show. Pat Hancock, hybridizer, described this large standard as having semidouble pink-lavender ruffled pansy blossoms with raspberry and purple fantasy and raspberry-purple edge. The foliage is variegated dark green, pink and cream, heart-shaped, glossy, with serrated edge and red back. Anne Thompson was the exhibitor.

'The Alps' (#7813–1992) was the Best Standard Chimera at the 2007 Show. Hybridized by K. Horikoshi and H. Sawara, this single-semidouble white pansy with light blue striped chimera blossom has medium green, plain, quilted foliage and is a standard. Susan Shaw exhibited this plant.

'Jolly Orchid' (#9719–2007) was the Best Miniature at the 2007 Denver Show. Described as having double orchid and white pansy blossoms over medium green, plain quilted foliage by hybridizer Hortense Pittman, this miniature plant was exhibited by Anne Nicholas.

'Ness' Cranberry Swirl' (#8134–1995) was Best Semiminiature at the 2007 show. Hybridized by the late Don Ness; Beverley Williams was the exhibitor. This plant is described as having double white star with variable fuchsia edge blossoms with variegated green and cream, plain, pointed foliage. While not officially a chimera, the description indicates sucker propagation is necessary.

'Shirl's Red Sky' (#9374–2004) received the award for the Best Shirley Sanders hybrid at the 2007 show. This award was in honor of the late Shirley Sanders as hybridizer of the Shirl's series of hybrids. This miniature plant has single light red pansy blossoms with white eye and variegated dark green and pink, pointed foliage. Catherine Thompson exhibited this plant.

3

'Foxwood Trail' (#6430-1986) received the award for Best Trailer at the 2007 show. Hybridized by T. Khoe and exhibited by Bill Price, this semiminiature trailer is described as having single variable pink with red center or fuchsia-pink with darker pink center blossoms. The foliage is plain green.

Saintpaulia ionantha was Best species at the Cincinnati Ohio convention in 2005. Beverley Williams exhibited this plant. *S. ionantha* is described as having single blue-violet blossoms, 4 to 5 per peduncle and very floriferous. It has dark green, pointed, heart-shaped foliage that tends to spoon. The foliage is also thick, quilted, glossy, slightly serrated, red back and has long red-brown petioles.

Saintpaulia grandifolia #299 received the awards of Best species and Second Best African violet in the 2007 show. Exhibitor was Bill Price. This species plant is described as having single dark blue-violet blossoms, one or more per peduncle and is very floriferous. The large foliage is light to medium green, elliptical, very thin, and crinkled, with long flexible petioles. It is usually grown as a single crowned plant.

'The King' (#2675–1975) was the Best Vintage Violet in the 2006 show. This plant, hybridized by the late Max Maas, was one of Pauline Bartholomew's favorites (page 14). Exhibited by Ken Rein, this standard size plant is described as having double dark blue-purple blossoms on plain foliage. Refer to page 15 for a description of Vintage Violets.

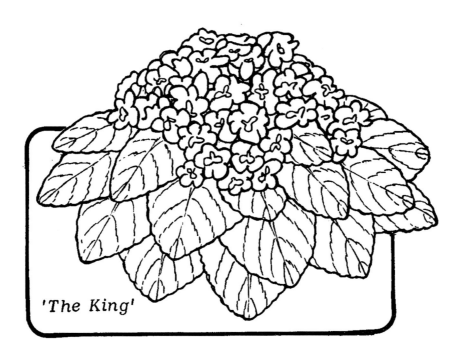

'The King'

Photographer, Tom Glembocki
AVSA Library Committee

Cover and photo page designs, Janet McDowell
www.lilliesatticphotography.com

Alliance

Rebel's Rose Bud

The King

Tropical Heat Wave

Buckeye Especially Mine

The Alps

Jolly
Orchid

Ness'
Crandberry
Swirl

Shirl's
Red Sky

Foxwood
Trail

Saintpaulia
Ionantha

Saintpaulia
Grandifolia

Any seasoned violet enthusiast can define *chimera, petiole, peduncle, tailored, wasp, longifolia, supreme,* and quite a lot more; but when you listen to the comments from visitors and new violet growers at any show you hear questions: "What's the difference between a miniature and a semiminiature?" "What makes this one a trailer?" "What's a sucker?"

If you are new to the violet world, this section is for you; if you are a long-time show grower, you might want to skip this section, or refer to it as you are called upon to mentor a new grower.

PLANT TYPES

The terms *variety* and *cultivar* are often used interchangeably to describe any African violet that is different from another which results from hybridization or as a *sport* or *mutant*. (A sport is a plant that shows a marked change from the parent plant; usually a natural mutation.)

The following types of African violets are recognized by AVSA and are bred by hybridizers as a specific type:

Standards

Standard refers to the size of a mature, *single-crowned* African violet cultivar with large leaves, which at maturity exceeds 8" in diameter. A *large* standard measures over 16" but can be as large as 20" to 24" in diameter. There is no differentiation between the two in judged shows; they are both classified as standards. The genetics of the variety, as well as growing conditions, dictate the ultimate size of a standard plant.

Single-crowned: A plant with a single center of growth from which foliage emanates in a *rosette* form. (*Rosette:* a cluster of leaves radiating symmetrically from a central stem.)

Miniatures and Semiminiatures

AVSA designates two sizes for small-growing, compact, single-crowned plants with small leaves: miniature and semiminiature. Miniatures must be six inches or less in diameter to be entered in the miniatures classes at AVSA Standard Shows; semiminiatures must be eight inches or less. The hybridizer designates the size of a variety.

Trailers

Trailers are genetically disposed to produce multiple crowns. African violet trailers range in size from micro-minis (leaf size approximately 1/4" x 1/2"); miniatures (leaf size approximately 1/2" x 1"); semiminiatures (leaf size approximately 1" x 1-1/2"); and, standards (leaf size over 1-1/2").

There are two forms of trailers: those with elongated stems that trail down around the pot, and those with short stems whose foliage forms bushy mounds. There are no size limits for trailers, but they must have at least three crowns coming from the main stem to be entered in a show.

Saintpaulia Species

African violet species are the ancestors of all cultivars and have provided the genetic material for hybridizing. Some species tend to be single-crowned, others are naturally multiple-crowned and still others are trailers. The quantity of blossoms varies greatly, with some species having many blossoms (floriferous) and others having few (rare) blossoms. Species must be looked at as native or wild plants, and, as such, they should be exhibited as they are, without artificial pruning.

Originally, twenty-seven species were classified and registered by AVSA. Recent DNA studies have provided new information and a new taxonomy. It has now been established that there are only six true species with a number of subspecies radiating from one of those six.

PLANT PARTS

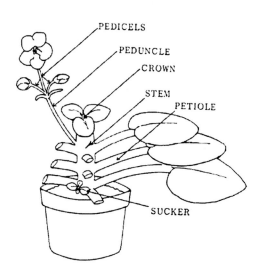

The following plant parts are referred to frequently in later sections of this book:

Crown: The head of the plant above the soil line. African violets are described as having single or multiple crowns.

Pedicel: The stem emanating from the peduncle and supporting the individual blossom in a flower cluster.

Peduncle: The stem emanating from an axil and supporting the entire flower cluster.

Petiole: The stem that connects the blade of the leaf to the crown.

Axil: The angle formed at the juncture of the petiole and the main stem.

Stem: The main stalk or trunk of a plant.

Sucker: The beginning of a new plant, which forms near the base of a plant or in the lower axils. For judging purposes in an African violet show, a sucker is not counted as such unless it shows four leaves and no sign of a bud. A sucker on a single-crowned specimen plant disqualifies it from being entered in a show since the plant is no longer considered to have a single crown.

BLOSSOMS

Blossom types are described in the *African Violet Master List (AVML)* as single, double, and semidouble. Blossom type is one of several ways African violets are classified for competitive showing.

The shapes of blossoms (e.g., pansy, star, cup, bell, wasp) are blossom type variations.

Blossom color patterns and descriptive features (e.g., eye, tips, fantasy, edged, Geneva edged, chimera, multicolor, pinwheel, two-tone) are another way in which African violets are classified for competitive showing. The *AVML* gives the official color description of the varieties, which is usually furnished by the hybridizer.

In addition to the blossom characteristics illustrated on the following page, several descriptive adjectives (e.g., large, mottled, variable, sticktite, ruffled, frilled, fluted) are used in blossom descriptions in the *AVML*.

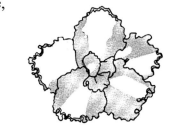

Blossom Types

Double: Two or more complete corollas with multiple lobes and anthers. (A *corolla* is the unit formed by the lobes or petals of a blossom.)

Semidouble blossom: A blossom with one corolla (five lobes). Sometimes two or more additional lobes form a tuft or crest in the center of the blossom.

Single: A fused corolla with five lobes and a single pair of anthers.

Blossom Shapes

Bell: Single blossoms with a bell shape.

Pansy: Blossoms have five lobes. The two upper lobes will be smaller than the lower lobes. The blossoms can be single, semidouble or double.

Star: Blossoms have five lobes of about equal size and distance from one another. The blossoms can be single, semidouble or double. The double star has extra layers of petals, but maintains the star form.

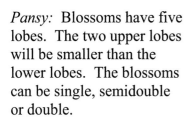

Wasp: Blossoms are single and each lobe is very narrow.

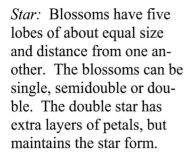

Blossom Color Combinations

Chimera: Blossoms with stripes of contrasting colors, that radiate from the center. It is also called a pinwheel blossom. Plants with true chimera blossoms will not propagate true from leaf cuttings and must be propagated from suckers, blossom stalks, or tissue culture.

Edged: Blossom can be any shape. Lobes of the blossoms are edged with any color. *Geneva edges* have all lobes edged with white.

Fantasy: Blossoms are splotched, streaked or rayed with contrasting color or a deeper shade of the same color. The blossoms can be of any kind or shape.

Fringed: Blossoms have heavily serrated or fringed outer lobes. The blossoms can be of any kind or shape.

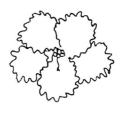

Multicolor: Blossoms with two or more distinctly different colors; often the upper lobe color differs from the lower lobes or "paw print" patterns on all lobes.

Two-tone: Blossoms have two or more shades, usually light and dark values, of the same color.

Foliage Types

African violet foliage ranges in color from light green through a dark mahogany green. Some dark green foliage may appear to have a red back. Foliage types are designated as *green* or *variegated*. Besides color, the shapes and textures of leaves are also distinctive. The more common foliage types:

Compound, Wasp, Bustle or Piggyback: Leaves are compound with one large and two smaller lobes. *Bustle-back* leaves have the back folded to the underside of the leaf to form a ruffled "bustle."

Girl: Deeply scalloped leaves usually rounded or heart-shaped with white to yellow markings at the base of each leaf. Markings can extend to the leaf blades and edges of the leaf.

Holly: Heavily crested leaves with leaf edges curled forward or bent back with exaggerated waxy edges resembling holly leaf.

Longifolia or Spider: Narrow, pointed, strap-like leaves with either plain or wavy edges.

Plain or Tailored: Plain in texture and form, it is sometimes known as standard or *boy-type* foliage.

Pointed: Ends of the leaves come to a definite point.

Quilted: Leaves have a distinct, raised area between the veins. Some leaves have piecrust edging.

Ruffled, Fringed, Wavy or Fluted: Leaves have serrated or ragged edges. *Ruffled* leaf edges resemble that of a ruffle and may appear "curly." *Wavy* leaf edges have a slight wave or rippled pattern.

Serrated: Slightly quilted, pointed leaves with noticeably serrated or saw-toothed edges.

Spooned, Ovate, Cupped-up: Leaves are concave with high edges like a spoon. The basic shape of an *ovate* leaf is of an egg with the largest end at the juncture of the petiole and leaf.

Supreme: Leaves are thick, hairy and quilted with strong pencil-like petioles. This term is also used to describe the entire plant.

Variegated foliage: Defines all variegation other than crown and mosaic variegation.

Variegated: Leaves (in addition to shades of green) can be marked with white, cream, light yellow or rosy shades from light pink to deep wine red. The different patterns of variegation may appear in random form or along leaf edges. A line of variegation around the edge of the leaf is referred to as "Tommy Lou" variegation.

Crown variegation has a variegated center crown surrounded by increasingly darker green leaves at the edge. Young leaves become greener as they age.

Mosaic variegation has shades of green mottled, splashed or mixed with white, cream, yellow or pink (a.k.a. "Lillian Jarrett").

It is easy to describe the characteristics of a perfect show plant. However, it is not so easy to find varieties that will fulfill these ideals. Many varieties lack the requirements of a good, all-around show plant. In reality, we settle for somewhat less than perfection and apply our growing skills to overcome the imperfections.

THE IDEAL SHOW PLANT

For foliage, we look for sturdy petioles growing straight and evenly distributed around the main stem. We want perfectly overlapping rows of leaves with the outer row in the pattern of a circle. We hope for foliage that is not so sensitive that it will react adversely to slight changes in culture. For floriferousness we look for a variety that produces numerous bloom stalks. We want lots of medium-to-large blossoms but not so many that the foliage is obscured or spent blossoms are impossible to clip out. We want peduncles strong enough to hold blossoms over the foliage at the right height. And finally, in both blossoms and foliage, we look for clear, bright colors that remain stable.

FINDING SHOW-QUALITY VARIETIES

There are many ways to find varieties that will make good show plants, but you may have to be persistent in order to get a plant or leaf cutting actually in your possession. Attend judged shows and make a list of the most striking varieties. Add the recommendations of award-winning growers to your list. Observe the plants grown by those who use the same culture methods that you use and arrange to trade plantlets or leaf cuttings with them. Search plant sales, nurseries, catalogs, and advertisements in the *African Violet Magazine*. And finally, don't miss the fun of ordering plants by mail and testing them out for yourself.

ANNUAL BEST VARIETY LIST AND HONOR ROLL

AVSA publishes an annual "Best Variety List" in the November/ December issue of the *African Violet Magazine* and "The Honor Roll of African Violets" in the July-August issue. The compiler of the list solicits favorites from AVSA members. Each year, the top twenty-five favorites are listed. In order for a violet to be on the Honor Roll, a variety must have appeared on the Best Varieties list for three consecutive years.

Varieties on the Honor Roll for the years 1997-2007 listed with registration number and name of hybridizer include:

'Tomahawk' #7269 (K. Stork)
'Irish Flirt' #7577 (S. Sorono)
'Ode to Beauty' #7677 (Cox/B/ Johnson)
'Picasso' #6924 (M. Tremblay)
'Ness' Crinkle Blue' #8136 (D. Ness)
'Milky Way Trail' #7469 (J. Stahl)
'Ness' Satin Rose' #8144 (D. Ness)
'Powwow' #7708 (K. Stork)
'Rob's Sticky Wicket' #6467 (R. Robinson)
'Windy Day' #7719 (Stork/Boone)
'Rainbow's Quiet Riot' (R. Wasmund)
'Frozen In Time' #9167 (S. Sorano)
'Orchard's Bumble Magnet' # 8495 (R. Wilson)
'Rebel's Splatter Kake' #8694 (R. Bann)

Descriptions of the above-named varieties may be found in the *AVML* and in the *First Class* computer database. These varieties have won and continue to win awards at local, state, council and national shows.

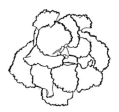

A Few of Pauline's 1985 Favorites

The following list of Vintage Violets selectively includes varieties from Pauline's 1985 personal Hall of Fame, several of which continue to be grown and shown. They are listed by registration date. The * denotes the plant was on the Honor Roll of Violets.

'TINY PINK' (#1648 – 1966) Lyndon Lyon, hybridizer. This tiny charming miniature was registered in 1966. A nosegay of double pink blossoms on miniature glossy strawberry foliage.

* 'MARY D' (#2675-1975) The late Max Maas, hybridizer. The Mona Lisa of show plants. Rather plain with understated beauty, yet it has had an enduring love affair with growers for all the years of her existence. Quietly unassuming with an enigmatic smile, she continues to win top awards. 'Mary D' has red semidouble blossoms on medium dark foliage and develops superbly perfect symmetry without even trying.

* 'THE KING' (#2698 – 1975) The late Max Maas, hybridizer. The foliage is emerald green with a soft, matte finish. It has perfect symmetry with masses of jewel-toned deep blue to purple blossoms held high and spaced evenly around the crown. The foliage is a little sensitive so that steady, consistent culture is a must or the leaves may break out in a rash.

'PINK STAR LOU' (#3304 – 1978) Harold Rienhardt, hybridizer. What a great performer this variety is. It loses leaves through natural attrition but the foliage keeps filling in. My plant took Best Standard Trailer at the 1985 AVSA convention in Los Angeles when it was three years old and had never been repotted nor had the soil ever been leached.

*'TIGER' (#3433 – 1978) Irene Fredette, hybridizer. This is an all-time favorite of growers and never fails to catch the eye of those who attend judged shows. It has dark green and white variegated foliage with tints of pink. The blossoms are dark, blue-violet semi-doubles. 'Tiger' soon outgrows a 5" pot and will grow huge when potted on to a 6" or 8" pot.

'LI'L CREEPER' (#3749 – 1979) Lyndon Lyon, hybridizer. One of the best variegated miniature trailers from one of the pioneers of miniature trailer hybridizing. Tiny leaves with well-formed foliage and dark pink double blossoms. It is a prolific bloomer and an all-time favorite of many growers.

*'MARIE KNOBLOCK' (#4042 – 1980) Barbara Sisk, hybridizer. This variety can look like an exotic shrub with a leaf span of 22" and outer leaves measuring 5" across and 6" long. The ruffled foliage is a deep emerald green frosted in pink and white and is crowned with a bouquet of large garnet red blossoms. This variety is very sensitive and the center burns easily. It wants less fertilizer and more leaching.

'RAMBLIN' PINK' (#4188 – 1980) Ethel Champion, hybridizer. This pink variegated charmer comes from the champion hybridizer of variegated varieties 'Ramblin' Pink' needs lots of strong light to maintain the pink in the variegation, which makes a gorgeous background for the double pink blossoms.

*'WINNERGREEN' (#4693 – 1981) Hortense Pittman, hybridizer. One of the better ruffled-type foliage semiminiatures. Lovely frilled, double white blossoms with green and lavender tints.

*'FISHERMAN'S PARADISE' (#4843 – 1982) Barbara Sisk, hybridizer. A very unusual pattern of "Tommie Lou" variegation. The leaves have random black - green splotches with occasional splashes of celadon green. The light areas are chalk white with blushes of rosy pink. This lavender-blossomed plant doesn't need to be in bloom to be spectacular. Another one of the big ones if given root room.

VINTAGE VIOLETS

Many older varieties continue to be seen in shows today and may be exhibited in the Vintage Violet class at AVSA Standard Shows. According to AVSA, for a variety to be considered "Vintage," it must have been introduced at least 25 years prior to the year it is to be entered in the vintage class. Many of our Vintage Violets are now difficult to find, which alerts the serious grower to the value of keeping the variety growing and in circulation. A list of most-wanted vintage varieties is listed in the *African Violet Magazine* and on the AVSA web site to aid those growers who are searching for ones they lost.

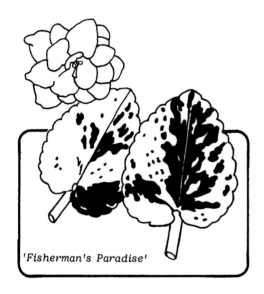

'Fisherman's Paradise'

TALLY TIME

"Tally Time," a summary of the varieties receiving the greatest number of total awards in AVSA Standard Shows throughout the year, is compiled and listed each year in the March-April issue of the *African Violet Magazine*. In addition to the number of awards the named varieties received in judged shows, this tally also lists the award winners by geographical regions. This information helps the grower choose show plants that adapt well in their area.

KNOW THE HYBRIDIZERS

Successful growers are as familiar with the name of the hybridizer of a variety as they are with the name of the variety. New growers soon begin to recognize the hybridizers and can watch for new introductions of those who have a good record for quality. Some hybridizers are noted for their work with miniatures, some specialize in variegated standards, and others are recognized for miniature trailers. Of course, many hybridizers produce quality introductions in a wide range of types.

The region where the plant was hybridized can make a difference. A variety that was hybridized in a cold dry region may grow very differently in a warm, humid climate or a dry hot one. It often takes time for some varieties, especially variegates, to acclimate to a new environment.

Praise and support the commercial growers who offer the releases of hybridizers who have a background of genetic knowledge, who work with strong, stable stock, and who offer consistently high-quality varieties. Protect us from the breeders who release and register every plant that jumps up from the seedbed, no matter how ordinary or duplicative it may be. These puny efforts become listed in perpetuity and eventually will make the *AVML* the size of a big city telephone directory.

Judges should encourage good hybridizing by not compromising judging standards to accommodate a plant's poor growth habits. Awards are meant to acknowledge the skill of the grower, but they are also an unspoken tribute to the skill of the hybridizer.

REGISTRATION OF AFRICAN VIOLETS

Registration of African violets began in 1949, and now the African Violet Society of America, Inc., has registered nearly 10,000 varieties. AVSA is the International Registration Authority for the genus *Saintpaulia* (African violet) as designated by the Council of the International Society for Horticulture Science. Only named varieties can be exhibited in AVSA shows, and only registered varieties can be entered for the AVSA Collection Awards.

To be eligible for registration, an African violet cultivar, produced originally either as a mutant or from seed, must be propagated vegetatively through three generations. (See *The Handbook For Growers, Exhibitors, and Judges* for more information.)

The *African Violet Master List of Species and Cultivars* (known as the *AVML,* formerly *MVL*) is compiled and published by the African Violet Society of America, Inc. All registered cultivars from the inception of registration (February 25, 1949) and all recognized species to the date of publication of the most recent edition are listed in the *AVML*. Additionally, unregistered cultivars appearing in previous editions and supplements to the *AVML* since 1983 are included. Each issue of the *African Violet Magazine* lists the most recent registrations.

'The King'

First Class (FC), a computer database that is updated six times a year by the Chairman of the AVSA Registration Committee, lists over 15,000 cultivars of which nearly 10,000 are registered varieties. *FC* has the most up-to-date listing of registered varieties. In addition to the registration information, which includes the name, description, hybridizer, and date of registration, photos of over 4,000 varieties are included.

The African Violet Master List of Species and Cultivars, *First Class*, and *The Handbook For Growers, Exhibitors, and Judges* are available from AVSA. Current price information for AVSA publications can be found in the most recent issues of the *African Violet Magazine* or from the AVSA website at www.avsa.org.

Experienced growers know how difficult it is to find three high-scoring, registered varieties for the AVSA Collection Class (See Selecting Entries, p. 90). Therefore, the largest percentage of plants in your collection should be registered. Because excellent show plants are sometimes not registered until a year or more after release, don't pass up a good variety because it is not registered. But be aware of how many registered varieties you have and check the *AVML* or *First Class* for new registrations.

'Falling Snow'

Whether you "grow to show" or grow just for your own pleasure, acquiring new plants is exciting and challenging. There are many blossom and foliage types, and the hybridizers keep trying for the new and different.

AVSA affiliates (clubs, councils) throughout the country hold shows and sales; most are listed on the Coming Events page of the AVSA website. Keep informed of shows within driving distance. Members of the affiliate organization sponsoring the show and sale are more than willing to help you choose plants and give you advice on caring for your plants. Better yet, look for an affiliate near you and join. There is no better place to learn and share information and acquire new varieties.

MAIL-ORDER VIOLETS

Reading variety descriptions in advertisements is an exciting guessing game. It is only natural for merchants to extol the virtues of their products. Growers must learn to read between the lines and become familiar with the style of advertising copywriters.

When some suppliers describe a variety as "show quality," you can count on it. Others do not mean to deceive; it's just that their standards are lower!

And then there is the interpretation of blossom size. Blossoms are described as big, large, huge, and giant – never small or medium. If the description merely says "very showy blossoms," one might wonder what is wrong with the foliage.

Many commercial growers of African violet are AVSA commercial members and advertise in the *African Violet Magazine;* their e-mail and/or Internet addresses and phone numbers are easily

available. Some have extensive catalogs (with pictures) on their websites, and/or they will mail you their catalogs–some free, some for a small fee. Shipping of plants and leaves is seasonal and the suppliers take this into consideration when filling orders.

If you decide to order from sources other than established commercial growers, proceed with caution, especially with Internet auctions. Most reliable commercial growers state their prices on their websites. Visit the sites and get an idea of fair pricing. Even more important: good commercial growers will label their plants accurately, charge reasonable prices, pack them well for shipping, and you will have recourse if you have problems with your order.

UNPACKING PLANT ORDERS

When new growers receive their first mail-order shipments, they expect to open the box and pull out perfect little plantlets in full bloom. But plants just don't ship in that kind of condition; they are usually rolled in a cylinder of newspaper or cardboard, and, while there may be lots of foliage, it is usually leggy and floppy. There may or may not be blossoms. Fairly soon, however, the grower learns that the shipment will pay big dividends. Outer leaves are removed and put down for propagation; plantlets are potted up into 4" pots, and in a few months they will be well formed with full foliage. So the grower gets far more than just one plant for the money.

UNPACKING PLANTS: Unwrap the plants carefully, removing all plastic wrapping and tape. As you work, keep track of plant name-tags and check names against the order (there may be substitutes or gift leaves). Don't forget to make out records for each variety for your files.

UNPACKING LEAVES: Unwrap leaves carefully to avoid breaking petioles. Follow the directions for propagating leaf cuttings.

All newly acquired plants, no matter from what source, should be potted up immediately if they are large enough and in good condition. The sooner they are potted according to your methods and in your potting mix, the faster they will adapt to your conditions. Follow the instructions on Potting Up Plantlets (p. 59) and Propagation (p. 65). For some plants, you may need to follow the guidelines for Trauma Care (p. 62). Regardless of the source, follow all precautions! (See Pests, Pathogens, and Physiological Problems (p. 111).

LIMIT YOUR COLLECTION

Many new growers buy more plants than they have time to care for and put down every leaf that breaks off. Soon their space is overflowing.

One of the biggest mistakes new growers make is in adding more light stands to keep up with the number of plants they accumulate. This only postpones the inevitable, because eventually the saturation point is reached through the limitations of budget and time.

Set your limit from the beginning and stick to it, no matter how great the temptation is to expand. Make the plants fit the space; don't expand the space to accommodate the plants. If your life style changes (you may retire, for example), you can rethink your position.

If you are dedicated to growing for competition, 50 to 60 plants are the most you should attempt to care for. From a collection of that size, it is possible to enter up to 36 standard-sized plants in one show. It doesn't take a lot of time to attend to that number, but their needs must be met at the proper times. If time is stretched much further, show plants will very likely be neglected.

Group the varieties together with the best show plant potential; give these plants the best location in the house and first call on your time. Few growers can manage to be both quantity growers and award winners. Only you can decide what your goal is.

Anyone growing African violets for show (and also those who are just growing for pleasure) should keep a record of all varieties in his/her collection. It will be needed for a number of reasons.

1. It makes it easier to fill out a pre-entry sheet when participating in a judged show. The description and registration number need not be looked up each time if they are listed on a file card, spreadsheet or computer database.

2. If the variety name has been identified from a source other than an AVSA publication (such as a commercial catalog), that information can be furnished to the classification committee. Varieties not listed with any source may still be entered in a show, but the classification committee may question you about their origins.

3. If you or your source have mislabeled a plant, it will be easier to track down the error.

The official sources for the information to be entered in the records are AVSA publications: The *Africa Violet Master List*, *First Class*, and the Registration Report published in the *African Violet Magazine*. Unofficial sources are commercial catalogs, advertisements, and word-of-mouth. Make every effort to locate an official source.

THE RECORD SHOULD INCLUDE:

1. Where or from whom the variety was obtained, what form it was in (leaf, plantlet, mature plant), and the date it was acquired.

2. The full, proper name of the variety.

   Many hybridizers use a series name for their plants. For example: 'Lyon's Lavender Magic' (Sorano), 'Suncoast Lavender Magic' (W. Williams), and 'Lavender Magic' (H. Pittman) are three very different plants by three hybridizers. It is important to use the full name in your records.

3. The hybridizer's name, the registration number, and the date of registration. The new grower needs to become familiar with the names of hybridizers.

4. The registration number must be given for all plants that are entered in the AVSA collection classes. The registration date indicates when the variety was registered but not necessarily when it was released for sale.

5. It is best for the official description to be worded exactly, but if the wording is not available, consult advertisements or fall back on own observation. Be sure to include the leaf type and the plant size (standard, large, etc.).

6. Additional notes should include the first source of the information. If more information is obtained, add it with the uppermost listing representing the current information. The first notation for a new variety may even be "NL" (not listed) indicating that an attempt to find a listing has been made and that the search will continue.

FILING TIPS: Group these together alphabetically under separate headings: variegated standards; plain foliage standards; miniature and semiminiature single-crowned; and miniature, semi miniature, and standard trailers. When a variety is eliminated from your collection, date the record and retire it to a section in the back of the file (in alphabetical order) for possible future reference. The reason the variety was retired may also be noted.

The *First Class* computer database allows for the inclusion of a short note for each variety in the database where you can (a) enter pertinent information on each plant in your collection, and (b) sort the database for varieties that have your notes. It also includes the option for a user database where you can enter new varieties that are not yet listed in the database. Several search and print options are included. More information on can be found on the AVSA website.

The Psychology of Growing

Practice psychology–on yourself and your African violets. When you enter your plant room the sight should delight your senses. If you see well-grown plants groomed to perfection, you are more inclined to take good care of them. If you see a mess, it is easy to become discouraged and neglectful.

Let dust balls gather under the beds and dishes stack up in the sink, but keep a tidy plant room. Every one of us is a goodwill ambassador for African violets, and every visitor is a potential convert; show them shining foliage, fresh blossoms and a reasonable semblance of order, and then hear the gasps of amazement. Show them untidy plants, a hodge-podge of leaf cuttings and growing paraphernalia, and the African violet will take a step backward.

Talk to your plants. Show plants are like show people; under the right direction they give an outstanding performance. But you do have to admire them, applaud them, and tell them they are beautiful.

You will also need to talk to other people *about* plants, which is why there is such an advantage in belonging to an African violet club. Just try to talk about plants with non-growers; their eyes glaze over and roll back in their heads. We seek relief by joining horticultural clubs. There we can find a room full of people who understand exactly how we feel when we get ecstatic over a new variety.

Keep yourself and your African violets properly "psyched up" and you will have taken the first step toward growing prize-winning plants.

Tips For Casual Growers

- Use a potting and watering method that best suits your needs and life style.

- Use a good quality soilless potting mix. Compare prices. As the old saying goes, "you usually get what you pay for." Unless the mix shows a high proportion of perlite, add one part perlite to three parts mix.

- Provide light, light, light, and don't over-pot.

- If you are not inclined to follow the procedure of potting down a neck, discard the plant when it begins to look like a palm tree and replace it with a fresh new plant.

- Even after the casual grower has achieved success in growing healthy plants, the persistent complaint is, "I can't get my African violets to bloom." The main causes for lack of bloom are listed in the order of their importance. Check the Table of Contents for the culture methods mentioned.

    o Inadequate light is the most important factor in lack of bloom.

    o Either lack of fertilizer or too infrequent fertilizing is next in importance. Use a dilute fertilizer solution each time the plants are watered.

    o Over-potting is another factor. If over-potted, the plant puts all its energy into forming new roots. When the roots are slightly restricted, more energy goes into forming blossoms. Keep plants in pots no larger than 4" or 5" in diameter.

    o Finally, multiple crowns (suckers) can form such a mass of foliage that the light is shut out of the centers (crowns). Keep single-crowned varieties single-crowned by removing suckers as soon as they form.

Get organized. Make it convenient to pot, groom, and water. You will find yourself procrastinating if supplies must be collected from various storage areas before you can start to work. Put all the potting tools in a plastic tray or handled carrier. Set aside a cabinet in the kitchen (or wherever you will be potting) in which to store the tool tray, a basic supply of pots, and a pail of potting mix.

TOOLS

Many of these tools are in everybody's toolbox. After you have been working with plants for a while you will find that you use some more than others and you will probably discover a few new favorites of your own.

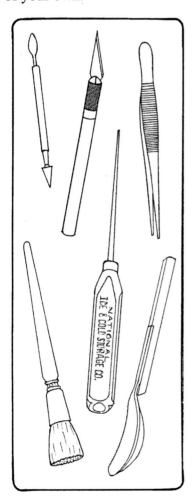

BRUSHES: A soft, 1" brush for whisking soil from petioles, leaves, and pots. A small 1/4" brush for daubing rooting powder on freshly scraped long necks.

CALENDAR: A wall calendar with plenty of space for writing notes, recording repotting dates, application of pesticides, and show plant disbudding schedule.

FERTILIZER JUGS: Use gallon jugs for storing fertilizer solution. They are good for keeping a handy supply of room temperature water. One-gallon bleach bottles, thoroughly rinsed, are suitable because they are opaque. Clear plastic jugs will develop an algae build-up unless you use an algaecide in the water. Milk jugs are easily replaced; throw them out when they get "green" with algae.

LEAF SUPPORT RINGS: See Training For Symmetry, p. 74.

ICE PICK: If you can still find one, it will be useful for lifting root balls out of large pots. When heated, it can be used for making small holes in plastic pots.

KNIVES: You will need one knife, preferably serrated, long enough to cut through an 8" root ball and a smaller knife to scrape scar tissue from long necks. The butt-end can be used to tamp soil mix between pots when mold potting.

MAGNIFYING GLASS: Useful for reading the fine print on fertilizer and pesticide bottles and to check for thrips.

MAGNIFYING LOUPE: At least 20x magnification for identifying mites and other pests. Available from scientific or photographic supply stores. Also known as a jewelers' loupe. A *must* to help identify the tiniest of pests.

MARKING PEN: Black, waterproof marking pen for writing variety names on a removable label or piece of tape applied to the pot or writing on the pot itself. This type of pen will write on slick, smooth surfaces.

MATTING MATERIAL: Many things will work: acrylic blanket material, pressed-fiber synthetic carpeting (without rubber backing), acrylic felt or fleece, or commercial matting.

MEASURING SPOONS: Reserve a set for the plant room for measuring fertilizer, pesticides.

NEWSPAPER OR POTTING TRAY: This will help keep your workspace clean. Wrap old soil and leaves in newspaper for the trash; use fresh sheet of newspaper for each plant.

NUT PICK: Either the rounded end or the pick end is the right shape for a multitude of purposes: lifting up root balls when repotting, tucking roots of plantlets into a potting hole, poking holes in mix for leaf cuttings or heating to poke holes in pots.

ONE-QUART MEASURES: These are for measuring potting mix components. A one-pound coffee can or yogurt container makes a free one-quart measure.

RAZOR BLADES: To cut petioles for leaf cuttings, use a single-edged stainless steel blade (only eight to ten times, then get a new one). Or, use a graphic arts X-Acto® knife; replace the blade before it gets dull.

REFERENCE BOOKS: See African Violet Society of America, Inc., publications, p. 115.

SCISSORS: Small, fine-cutting ones (such as manicure scissors) for close trimming of the pedicels of spent blossoms; regular scissors for cutting wicking material, labels, etc.; long-handled, surgical-type scissors for cutting peduncles at the main stem of the plant. Check with a friend in a medical profession; hospitals and clinics use disposable ones for cutting bandages.

SOLDERING IRON (electric): To make holes in pots for Texas potting and plastic cups.

SPOONS: You will need a few different sized spoons for scooping potting mix and adding mix under the leaves. Baby spoons work great for miniatures.

SPRAYER: One-quart size or larger with an adjustable nozzle for fine-mist spraying.

SPONGE: A natural sponge about the size of a small orange (larger ones may be cut to size). See Grooming, p. 76. Check the advertisements in the *African Violet Magazine* or try ceramic hobby shops or cosmetic departments to find natural sponges.

SUCKER PLUCKER: This handy little gadget is advertised in the *African Violet Magazine* or may be found in ceramic hobby shops. It has an oval end for scooping small, unwanted suckers out of leaf axils. The triangular end slips between sucker, petioles, and the main stem to remove wanted suckers intact for propagation.

TWEEZERS: Long tweezers (about 7") will reach into the dense foliage of trailers to remove spent blossoms and petioles.

WATERING CANS: A more precise amount of water can be poured with a long-spouted can, but a short-spouted can pours faster. You might want both kinds.

SUPPLIES

BLEACH: Liquid chlorine bleach for sanitizing purposes. A container of 10% bleach solution to be used for cleaning knives, etc.

FERTILIZERS: See Fertilizing, p. 46.

FLUORESCENT TUBES: See More Details About Tubes (p. 29) for information on types of fluorescent tubes.

LABELS: Sticky labels are available from office-supply stores in a variety of sizes; get some that fit your pots and your handwriting.

LYSOL® DISINFECTANT SPRAY: Keep on hand for sanitation and as a fungicide. It is available in aerosol cans and concentrated liquid.

MASK AND GLOVES: Use a molded painter's masks and disposable gloves when mixing soil and spraying for pests.

PESTICIDES: See Pesticide Arsenal, p. 111.

pH TESTING EQUIPMENT: See pH, p. 39.

PLASTIC BAGS: Small sandwich bags or snack size bags for bagging leaves, suckers, small plants and other sizes for various purposes. A roll of clear plastic or dry cleaner bags for tenting plants when re-rooting crowns, starting plantlets, and leaves.

PLASTIC BOXES (CLEAR): Containers of different sizes that can be tightly closed when high humidity is needed; for intensive care when rooting crowns and leaves.

PLASTIC CUPS: 3-ounce Solo® plastic drinking cups are economical for putting down leaves, potting up plantlets, and storing show-plants. (Be sure to make holes in bottom of cups for drainage.)

POTS: See Pots (p. 24) for sizes and types.

POTTING MIX INGREDIENTS: See Potting Mix, p. 41.

ROOTING POWDER: Rooting powder or hormone with fungicide can be used on freshly scraped long necks and to root suckers and blossoms stems. (Use is optional.)

SCREENING: Some pots may have extra large holes. A piece of nylon screen in the bottom of the pot will keep the perlite from coming through the holes. It will also make it easy to push a root ball out of a pot. Nylon won't rust and may be reused indefinitely.

STARTER MIX: Keep a bag of leaf start mix in the plant room so leaves may be put down as desired when they are removed during grooming. See Propagation, p. 65.

SUPERTHRIVE®: A concentrated source of various vitamins, hormones, and other ingredients; used to prevent transplant shock. Also added to fertilizer solution for the general health of plants. Its use is optional; many growers do not use this product.

WICKING MATERIAL: Acrylic yarn (be sure it isn't treated to be water repellent), nylon seine cord, polyester 1/8" 4-ply upholstery cord (separated into 4 strands). Do not use cotton or wool yarn.

EQUIPMENT

AIR CONDITIONER: If seasonal temperatures usually exceed 85°F, an air conditioner will be needed. Evaporative coolers are suitable for use in low humidity areas and will provide additional humidity. Refrigerated air conditioners deplete moisture in the air so that humidity needs to be supplemented.

DEHUMIDIFIER: Use a dehumidifier when humidity is over 70% for long periods of time.

FAN: A small fan will provide air movement in the plant room.

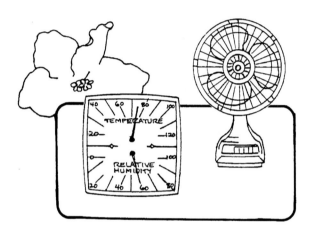

FLUORESCENT LIGHT STANDS: See Lighting section, p. 27.

FLUORESCENT TUBES: Keep a supply of fluorescent tubes on hand. Usually less expensive if bought by the case. See More Details About Tubes, p. 29.

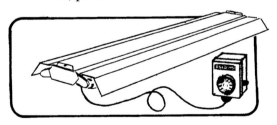

48" FLUORESCENT 2-TUBE FIXTURE: An additional fixture is handy for leaf cuttings and other miscellaneous items. Suspend from the ceiling by chains or purchase a free-standing tabletop model.

GAUGES: Combination hygrometer (for measuring relative humidity) and thermometer gauges are inexpensive. Place two or more in various locations in the plant room. See Humidity, p. 37.

HEATING: It is hoped that your existing home heating system will keep the temperature from dropping below 60°F in the plant room. If not, you may want to consider using a small electric heater to supplement the heating system. Check local codes.

HUMIDIFIER: Use a humidifier in dry localities or for occasional dry-weather conditions. Use a cool-air humidifier in the summer and a steam humidifier in the winter.

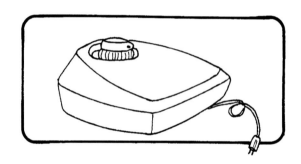

TIMERS: Plug all fluorescent fixtures into timers for consistent control of light hours.

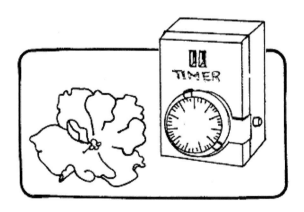

TRADEMARKS AND BRAND NAMES: Mention of a trademark or brand name of a proprietary product does not constitute an endorsement of the product by AVSA.

POTS

For African violets, clay pots have gone the way of the dinosaur. They were used in the early days of growing violets because they were porous and roots could breathe. When plastic pots appeared on the market, growers soon started using them because of their many advantages. They are lightweight, inexpensive, and easily sterilized. Clay pots are just the opposite, plus they have the added problems of algae and salts build-up and rapid water loss. However, growers had to rethink growing procedures in order to keep the fussy roots of African violets happy in a non-porous container.

This opened up a whole new field. Manufacturers worked to improve pot designs and growers developed lighter soil mixes and methods that would enable African violets to be grown successfully in plastic pots. As a result, giant strides have been made. We now have the benefit of unique new pot designs.

Utility Pots

You will need to know the terminology of utility pot sizes. If only one measurement is given, it refers to the diameter of the pot. If an additional measurement is given, it refers to the depth of the pot. However, the depth of a pot is not usually specified. Short utility pots suitable for African violets are referred to as "tub," "squatty," "azalea," or "bulb pan." Tall utility pots are referred to as "standard."

Manufacturers' standards for pot sizes are generally as follows, but different brands may vary somewhat. Square pots are measured diagonally.

STANDARD: the depth is equal to the diameter.

TUB or AZALEA: the depth is equal to three-fourths of the diameter.

BULB PAN: the depth is equal to one-half of the diameter.

THUMB POT: 1-1/2 inch round used for micro-miniature violets.

Because African violets have shallow, fibrous roots, it is important to provide a shallow potting medium, which may require some creativity with standard pots. Since the inch or so of space at the bottom of the pot is unused by the roots, the soil stays wet and soggy. Thus, much of the aeration to the roots is cut off. You probably have heard of plants that don't like "wet feet" – well, African violets head the list.

African violets will tolerate a lot of moisture at their roots if the extra depth of the pot is filled with perlite instead of potting mix. It makes all the difference in the world when conditions are created where roots can *breathe*. Using a porous potting mix usually provides aeration for most container-grown plants (See Potting Mix, p. 41). However, even when planted in shallow pots, the root system of African violets benefits from additional aeration.

Standard pots can be used for Texas-Style potting by using a deeper perlite layer and adjusting the water level and watering intervals. However, tub pots are usually used for growing show plants. The proportion and balance are more pleasing when exhibiting plants and there is a wider margin for error in watering. The growth rate is greatly accelerated because of the greater utilization of nutrients by a healthier, more extensive root system.

Texas-Style potting/watering will be discussed in the section on watering (p. 54). This style of potting uses a deep layer of perlite in the bottom of the pot. Holes are made in the sides of the pot at the top of the perlite layer for watering and aeration of roots.

Basic Tub Pots

An entire collection of African violets may be grown exclusively in tub pots. However, the specialty pots used in conjunction with tub pots will add a dimension of convenience and attractiveness. The following information serves as a general guide to pots.

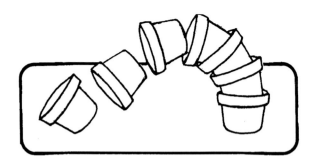

TUB POTS - SIZES

2-1/2" pot: Use this size when putting down leaves and potting up plantlets from leaf cuttings. Also, use this size for miniature and semiminiature single-crowned varieties. Since the soil dries out rapidly, watering is easier if the pots are placed on trays and watered together.

4" pot: Use this size when potting up standard, single-crowned plantlets from a 2-1/2" pot (6" to 8" diameter leaf span). Observe the plant in this size pot for two months or so in order to determine the growth habits, floriferousness, and general show plant potential. It is also suitable for bush-type or true-trailing miniature and semiminiature trailers. Single-crowned standards may be exhibited in this size, but the foliage would be limited to 12" or 13" in diameter (See Pot-to-foliage Proportions, p. 88).

5" and 6" pots: Use these sizes for large standard, single-crowned show plants. They are also suitable for large-growing, true-trailing miniature and semiminiature trailers.

7" and 8" pots: Use these sizes to grow a few single-crowned giants (20" or more). Use varieties classified as "large." However, some varieties classified as "standard" will, by leaf size and growth habits, indicate a potential for growing large. Of course, if your space is limited, all varieties—standard or large—may be kept restricted to a 4" to 6" pot.

TUB POTS - LAYER DEPTHS

The layer depths of perlite and potting mix depend on the size of the pot and the personal preference of the grower. Some growers prefer not to use a layer of perlite at the bottom of pots, especially small pots. Free space at the top also depends on the width and depth of the pot. The following is a guide:

2-1/2" pot: 1/2" perlite + 1-1/2" mix + 1/4" free top space = 2-1/4" total depth.

4" pot: 1" perlite + 1-3/4" mix + 3/4" free top space = 3-1/2" total depth.

5" pot: 1" perlite + 2-1/4" mix + 3/4" free top space = 4" total depth.

6", 7", 8" pots: 1-1/4" perlite + 2-1/2" mix + 3/4" free top space = 4-1/4" total depth.

Other Pot Types

In addition to the basic utility pot, other styles of pots and reservoirs (such as Dandy Pots, Optimara Watermaid, Volkmann's Reservoir Wick Pots) are designed for wick watering. A variety of plastic wick water reservoirs are available for use with tub pots. Swift's Moist-Rite plastic planter/reservoirs are designed for constant watering. The Oyama Planter, originally designed for bottom watering has evolved into a self-watering pot; it is discussed in detail in the section on watering (p. 55). The above pots and reservoirs are available from commercial vendors who advertise in the *African Violet Magazine.* Each type serves a purpose for growing prize-winning specimens.

Lighting

As a rule, African violets are happy in the same atmosphere in which people are comfortable; not too hot, not too cold, fresh air, but no drafts; enough humidity to keep tissues moist; and enough light in which to flourish. But, creating maximum conditions for raising show-quality plants requires extra effort.

The first priority is to give the plants a room of their own so that conditions are easier to control. If necessary, try for a sheltered corner of a kitchen or dining room that is free of dust and drafts of heavy traffic.

While natural light is satisfactory for the casual grower, a series of cloudy, rainy days could put plants out of the running for an entire show season. Only artificial light can provide the precise conditions required for show plants. So the next step is to choose the best equipment for fluorescent-light growing.

FLUORESCENT LIGHT GROWING

Many growers use standard shop fluorescent fixtures and home-built light stands made of wood, PVC pipe, or adaptations of commercial shelving. Some are marvels of ingenuity, but some are rather shaky and do not compare to the flexibility and quality of professionally manufactured light stands. Articles with instructions for building light/plant stands can be found in the *African Violet Magazine*. (Go to the *AVM Index* on the AVSA web site for articles on plant stands.)

A number of commercial light stands are available from vendors advertising in the *African Violet Magazine* and from horticulture product suppliers on the Internet. Most stands (often called grow-carts or light-carts) come complete with fixtures, are constructed from one-inch square aluminum, move smoothly on casters, have slide adjusting fixtures, and are easy to assemble. A variety of sizes are available.

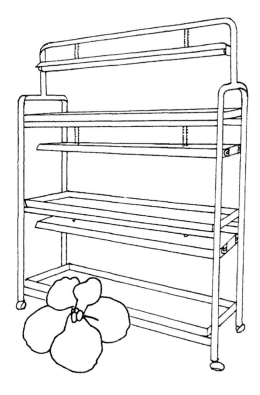

Such stands generally accommodate standard 11" x 22" trays. Ideally, the fixtures should have wide spacing between the tubes for maximize light distribution.

Tube Length & Light Efficiency

The efficiency of fluorescent tube sizes is a factor in the choice of light fixtures. The middle forty inches of a 48" tube and the middle sixteen inches of a 24" tube provide most of the light; the four inches from the ends of the tube are insufficient for optimum growth and flowering.

"Tube length" is a case where two plus two does not equal four. A 24" tube (for a small stand) costs as much or more than a 48" tube, lasts less than half as long, and does not equal its light intensity. Unless a narrow location needs to be lighted, avoid using 24" fixtures.

Fluorescent lights are the least expensive form of lighting. The power used by a double-tube, 48" fluorescent light fixture is the same as that of a single hundred-watt bulb.

If you wish to compute the actual cost of operating your light stand, multiply the total number of watts (multiply total tube wattage by the number of hours used per day). This gives the total number of *watt-hours*; then multiply the total watt-hours by the utility charge per kwh that appears on your electric bill. Divide by 1,000 to get the cost per kilowatt-hours (kwh) used per day. In simpler terms:

Cost per week equals:
$$\frac{total\ watts \times hrs\ /day \times cost\ per\ kwh}{1,000}$$

Understanding Fluorescent Lighting

These incredible stand-ins for sunlight enable the indoor gardener to have complete control of plant growth and flowering. Before fluorescent light, houseplants were at the mercy of the sun (will it shine today or not?) and the placement of windows in the home. When fluorescent lights became available, growers quickly discovered that they had a definite effect on growth and that plants could be grown exclusively under artificial light.

Getting into the technical side of artificial light is necessary to a point. The visible rays of the *spectrum* are a blend of red/orange, yellow/green, and blue/violet. White light (such as sunlight) is made up of a range of wavelengths. What we see as blue light is composed of the shorter wavelengths; red light is composed of longer ones. When combined in equal amounts, they appear as white light.

Plants do not use all of these wavelengths. Some invisible rays, such as infrared, can actually be harmful to plants. The blue and red rays of the spectrum are the ones that most influence plants; blues affect growth, reds affect flowering

In their search for more effective tubes for plant growth, manufacturers began applying different combinations of *phosphors* (chemical substances that emit light at different wave lengths) to the inner surfaces of fluorescent tubes. They ultimately arrived at a combination of blue and red ray producing phosphors that favorably

affected plant growth and flowering. They discovered that the higher the percentage of blue and red phosphors used, the less light that was emitted; therefore, it was necessary to restore some of the yellow/green phosphors in order to increase the lumen count. This research has led to new types of fluorescent tubes.

Plants are less affected by how *bright* the light appears to be (visible light intensity expressed as *lumens*) and more affected with the *energy* of the light. "Cool white" and "warm white" tubes are low-energy, with predominantly red and blue wavelengths. "Wide-spectrum" high-energy tubes emit mostly red, far-red, and blue wavelengths. The low-energy tubes are not less efficient than the wide-spectrums, but they need to be placed closer to the plants.

All light has an effect on the perceived color of objects; it is called a *color rendering index,* or CRI. Sunlight has a CRI of 100. A tube with a CRI above 70 makes colors more natural and vibrant, while tubes with low CRI will distort blossom colors. Labels on most tubes give the CRI.

African violets do well with ten to fifteen watts per square foot. Manufacturers of plant-growth-tubes recommend ten watts for propagation and fifteen watts for mature plants. A light cart that has one double-tube fixture over a shelf area of 20" by 48" provides twelve watts per square foot.

Since dust and grime reduce light output, keep tubes and undersides of reflectors wiped clean. Painting nearby walls a flat white can increase the effectiveness of available light. (Flat white has a greater reflective quality than does gloss white.) Mirrored walls also increase the efficiency of available light.

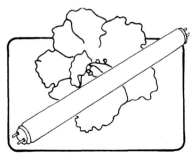

More Details About Tubes

Most types of florescent tubes can be found at home improvement stores such as Lowes and Home Depot. The following information should be helpful in making the right choice.

COOL WHITE & WARM WHITE

The terms "cool" and "warm" are not related to temperature but refer to the rays of blue and red emitted by the tubes. Ordinary shop lights, are *cool white* tubes; they produce some amount of red rays in addition to orange, yellow-green and blue, and they give a harsh light.

Warm white tubes, often referred to as soft white, have slightly more yellow and red and less blue and give a light that is warmer and less harsh. The combination of cool white and a warm white has the ability to simulate sunlight and to produce a sufficient range for African violets to thrive. These tubes are considerably less expensive than wide-spectrum, full-spectrum or other tubes designed for plants and aquariums.

In 1992, Congress passed an Energy Act, which required manufacturers to develop more energy-efficient lighting methods and supplies. Today's 34-watt tubes emit the same amount of light as the old 40-watt tubes. Since the new tubes are quite strong, it is important when replacing tubes to replace one tube in a fixture at a time or to reduce the hours per day to six or eight, gradually increasing one hour per day.

Other changes are occurring with fluorescent tubes. The designation "T12" is used in reference to 1-1/2" standard diameter tubes growers are most familiar with. A new 1" diameter tube now on the market is designated as "T8," and a 5/8" diameter tube as "T5." These will not work in most older fixtures, but newer fixtures are being manufactured that will accommodate both types.

Experiments show that maximum growth of most plants under cool white fluorescent lights will be equivalent to or better than that obtained under the blue-red phosphors; there is no advantage to the use of blue-red fluorescent tubes except for aesthetic purposes. (University of Alaska Cooperative Extension Service Bulletin HGA-00432)

SYLVANIA STANDARD GRO-LUX®

Sylvania developed the first fluorescent tubes for foliage plants in 1961. Sylvania *standard* Gro-Lux tubes are higher in the red and blue spectrums and give a red color to the plants. The tube itself gives off a purplish glow.

Under standard Gro-Lux the foliage appears to be a deeper green, and the color of blossoms and variegated foliage is more intense. Reds aren't as red, but appear to be a lovely deep magenta. Pink variegation that may not occur under high-energy tubes (such as the wide-spectrum tubes) will develop. The petioles of the plants are shorter, thicker and sturdier.

There is one small drawback: first-flowering and full floriferousness for show will take a little longer than for plants grown under high-energy, wide spectrum fluorescents.

Because of the lack of labeling information, it is difficult to identify tubes from other manufacturers with the same spectrum, lumens and CRI as the standard Gro-Lux tube. Tubes labeled for plant growth, if not marked as wide-spectrum, may be similar to the standard Gro-Lux tubes. Standard Gro-Lux tubes are more expensive than wide spectrum tubes.

Tube Type (40 watt)	Percentage of Plant Growth Rays		
	Red Rays	Yellow/ Green Rays	Blue Rays
Cool White	8.47%	42.94%	20.78%
Warm White	11.53%	43.41%	12.91%
Gro-Lux Standard	39.55%	15.44%	27.07%
Gro-Lux Wide-Spectrum	21.78% (8% far red) *	24.26%	14.29%

WIDE-SPECTRUM TUBES

Wide-spectrum fluorescent tubes were developed for high-energy plants, which include African violets. Wide-spectrum tubes have almost double the lumens and percentage of yellow/green rays of the standard Gro-Lux tube, plus additional rays in the far-red spectrum. The "plant growth" type wide-spectrum tubes emit a reddish glow. Wide spectrum tubes are referred to as high-energy tubes.

African violet foliage under wide-spectrum and other high-lumen combinations will actually, rather than just visually, be a lighter green. The blossom colors and coloring of variegated foliage will be less intense. Plants mature more rapidly, and flowering occurs earlier. Foliage will tend to reach toward the light, petioles and peduncles will elongate rapidly, and the pattern of growth will be more open.

These tubes were developed for accelerating growth in greenhouse-grown crops. They are best used in situations where plants receive some natural light, as in a greenhouse or near a window or in combination with standard Gro-Lux type or cool-white tubes. One wide spectrum and one cool white tube in each fixture will give a natural color to the plants. According to a Sylvania technical bulletin, high-energy plants like African violets seem to require more light in the far-red portion of the spectrum, and grow better if half of the lamps are standard Gro-Lux and half are wide-spectrum Gro-Lux.

Several manufacturers produce wide-spectrum tubes. If the tube is wide-spectrum, it will be printed on the tube near the ends.

FULL SPECTRUM TUBES

Full spectrum tubes are close to natural sunlight and are very effective for people with Seasonal Affective Disorder (SAD). Verilux®, Agro-Sun®, Ott Light® and other full spectrum fluorescents were engineered to reproduce all of the colors of the visible spectrum and a balance of natural light. These fluorescent tubes use a special blend of earth phosphors to create bright, balanced full spectrum light. Full spectrum tubes are available in 24" and 48" tubes and fit into standard fixtures. They are the most expensive of fluorescent tube types.

While some full-spectrum tubes are promoted "for seedlings, cuttings and high-energy plants like African violets," the grower should use them only in combination with a cool white tube.

Tube Replacement

Fluorescent tubes are bought for normal lighting purposes, burn for many years, and are not replaced until they burn out. However, tubes used for their effect on plant growth have limits.

Exhibitors of African violets operate on an annual show schedule, which is usually at the same time each year. To insure maximum bloom, one new tube should be placed in each fixture every year a few months before show. This means that each tube is replaced every two years. Be sure to write the date on new tubes (with a Sharpie felt-tip) just before they are put into the fixture.

Some growers only replace tubes when they burn out or when dark rings appear at the ends. Dark rings indicate a loss of effective energy and should be replaced immediately.

If both tubes are replaced at the same time, the sudden burst of energy will burn sensitive plants or you will see symptoms of too much light very quickly. Always save a few old tubes in the event this is ever necessary. Use an old tube in tandem with a new tube for a week and then replace it with the second new tube. If all new tubes are to be placed in a new light stand, start the light time at eight hours, increasing an hour each week until the appropriate number of hours is reached. Also, if possible, raise the fixtures for a few days.

LIGHT AND AFRICAN VIOLETS

African violets require red, blue, and yellow wavelengths of the color spectrum, variable amounts of light depending on the variety, and indeterminate day-length light requirements.

African violets are "high-energy" plants; high-energy plants require more light than low-energy plants such as philodendron and similar houseplants. Depending upon your violet setup, you can accomplish this by adding more tubes, adding reflectors above the fixtures to direct more light to the plants, moving the tubes closer to the plants or having the lights on for longer time periods per day.

If your plants receive some natural sunlight and there are white walls in the room the amount of light can be decreased from the fluorescent tubes proportionately.

Plant Day-Length Requirements

Plants are unique in that they are the only organisms that use light to convert certain elements into the food they require for growth and flowering. This process is called photosynthesis and plants have a wide range of photoperiodic (daylight) responses.

African violets are indeterminate-day plants; blooming is initiated under a wide variation of daylight hours (night neutral). They bloom in the short daylight hours of winter as well as in the long daylight hours of spring and summer. Plant lovers in temperate and tropical climates are fortunate that they can enjoy a wide range of flowering plants the year around. But in areas with long cold winters, you will see many homes with bright, blooming African violets in the windows.

Light Time For Plant Growth

Although African violets bloom in a wide range of light hours, growers do well to be more definite about the timing of light. If the room where

the light stands are located has quite a bit of natural light that ordinary house plants flourish, twelve to fourteen hours of fluorescent light is enough to maintain good growth and symmetry. If the room has little or no natural light, they will require fourteen to sixteen hours a day of fluorescent light. For maximum floriferousness, the light hours are increased on a schedule starting a few months before a show (See Pre-Show Schedule, p. 87).

Some growers who consistently have plants on the winner's table report they run lights 12 hours a day year round and do not increase light hours in preparation for show. Other growers use lights 10 to 12 hours for all plants most of the year and increase the light hours according to a schedule before show. Each grower must determine what works best under their growing conditions.

Plants need a dark period in order to form new flower stalks and should have at least six hours of darkness.

TIMERS: Always connect fluorescent lights to timers. A steady, consistent light program is important in growing show plants.

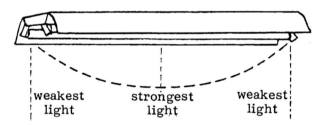

Plant Placement Under Lights

Not all varieties respond well to fluorescent growth lights. The foliage of a few varieties will grow gnarled and misshapen. If they are special varieties, you can try growing them further away from the lights. Having one fixture adjustable to 18" to 20" above the top of the plants is useful for placing problem plants until the foliage smoothes out. The light has to be lowered to the regular height eight weeks before show to bring the plants into full bloom.

Some plants do well at the ends of the tubes with the weakest light and others need the strongest light for maximum growth and blooming. Several species plants prefer less light and do well at the ends of tubes or in windows.

The following measurements refer to the distance between the tops of the plants and the bottom of the tubes:

- Leaf cuttings, plantlets, and miniatures should be about 6" to 8" below the lights. At 10" to 12" below the lights, plantlets and miniatures have a good growth rate and will stay flat and nicely shaped, but they will have few blossoms.

- Mature standard plants should be placed about 8" to 10" below the lights. Standard plants of some varieties will grow flat and compact with the tubes as high above them as 15" to 20", but the blossoms will be fewer than normal.

A phenomenon of plant growth called *phototropism* (reaching for the light) occurs whenever light intensity is stronger on one side of the plant. This growth pattern is often seen in a plant that has been placed near the end of the tube. To avoid this, rotate the plant every few days.

These placement recommendations are a general guide. There will be exceptions. Observe the reaction and growth pattern of the foliage. If the foliage of a variety that should normally lie flat is reaching upward, move the plant nearer the center of the lights or elevate it on an upturned pot. With experience you will find yourself automatically shifting plants around on the shelves in order to meet their needs.

VARIEGATED FOLIAGE

Temperature rather than light may be the most important factor in variegation. The cooler location of the bottom shelves (preferably no more than 70°F) is best for variegated varieties in the retaining of variegation. The higher the temperature, the greater the amount of nitrogen released from the soil and thus made available

to the plant. Excess nitrogen will result in the loss of some or all of the variegation.

NOTE: "Tommie Lou" type variegation is more stable under a wider range of conditions than crown variegation. Those varieties with crown variegation can lose almost all variegation in summer heat. However, the new leaves will start variegating again when cooler weather returns.

STACKING PLANTS

Space and differing light requirements is often a challenge, especially if light stand space is limited. By stacking plants on various-height risers, an amazing number of them can be grown on one shelf and still maintain the quality of prime show specimens. As many as eight intermediate-sized (12" to 16" diameter) or six of the giants (18" to 24" diameter) can be grown on one shelf. Place the elevated plants around the perimeter of the shelves so that the light emanating from the tubes will be blocked as little as possible.

If approximately two-thirds of the foliage of the lower-elevated plants receives good light, the symmetry and flatness of the growth is not affected. There is still ample circulation around the plants when they are elevated in this manner. The basic rule is that leaves must not touch. Leaves tend to curl or reposition themselves when the foliage of one plant touches that of another.

Too Much Or Not Enough Light?

Many people have tried remedy after remedy for poor performing plants and still end up bewildered. If you are having problems, are using appropriate fertilizer with which you are comfortable, and have eliminated the possibility of pests, it could be something as simple as lighting. Here are some general symptoms:

TOO MUCH LIGHT

1. The center of the plant will start producing smaller curled or knotted leaves, looking much like those with cyclamen damage.

2. The leaf color will become lighter and bleached looking. The edges may even start to dry out.

3. The shape of the leaf may change, causing ordinarily flat leaves to curl down around the pot or cupped leaves to flatten out.

4. Leaves with a red reverse may show a more intense coloration. It may also cause "birth-making" (reds splotches) on some leaves.

5. Variegated leaves may turn solid green.

If your plant shows these characteristics, try moving it toward the end of the tubes or other lower light location. A simple test for tight centers is to place a thin tissue over the center for several days to see if new growth improves.

NOT ENOUGH LIGHT

1. Plants will have very few blossoms and it takes a long time for new bloom stalks and blossoms to develop.

2. Rather than lying flat, petioles and leaves will start reaching for the light.

3. Leaves will be stunted resulting in a smaller than anticipated plant size.

If your plant shows these characteristics, try moving it toward the center of the tubes or other higher light location. You can also try stacking your plant to raise it closer to the light.

KNOW YOUR PLANTS

No rule is carved in stone with African violets. Although dark or light foliage may be predisposed to specific light requirements, there are always exceptions. Certain dark foliaged plants do best placed under the center of the tube. Certain light foliage will thrive in the lower light at the ends of the tube. Your plants will let you know; just watch them.

Summary: Fluorescent Light Growing

The type of tube, the watts per square foot, the distance from the plants, plant placement, and the light hours per day are all inseparable factors for the successful growing of African violet show plants under fluorescent lights. The following recommendations are a summary of those outlined in this chapter:

1. Use 20-watt (for 24" fixtures) or 40-watt (for 48 " fixtures) in one of the following configurations: one cool white tube and one warm white tube; one standard Gro-Lux tube combined with one cool white or one wide spectrum tube in each fixture.

2. Provide a minimum of 10 watts per square foot for propagation and 12 to 15 watts per square foot for mature plants.

3. Place the light tubes 8" to 10" above the foliage for mature standard plants and 6" to 8" for miniatures, plantlets, and seedlings.

4. Place variegated foliage on the cooler bottom shelves with heavily variegated varieties near the center of the tubes and lightly variegated varieties near the ends.

5. Run the fluorescent lights ten to twelve hours a day in rooms with good natural light and twelve to fourteen hours a day in rooms with little or no natural light. Connect the lights to timers.

MAINTENANCE OF FIXTURES

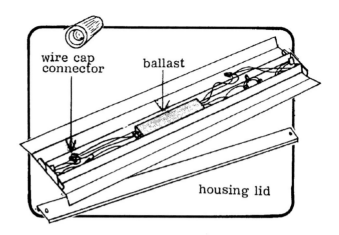

TUBES: If one tube in a double fixture is defective, the other tube will not fully light. First check the ends of the tubes for dark rings; the tube may be burned out. If there are no dark rings, try reseating the dark tube. Tubes sometimes work loose so the pins are not making proper contact.

If flickering and partial lighting occurs in both tubes when the lights first go on, it is probably condensation caused by the overnight accumulation of moisture. Wait an hour or so until the increase in room temperature and the heat from the ballast help dispel the condensation. If this is the problem, the tubes will light voluntarily.

Moisture will also sometimes corrode the metal pins so that they don't make proper contact. Gently sandpapering the pins will solve this problem.

FIXTURES: If both tubes of the fixture are dark, test them in another fixture. If they light, the problem is in the fixture. Some older fixtures require a starter; if the tubes aren't the problem, replace the starter. Even if you have had no experience as an electrician, there are two things you can do before you call for help.

LOOSE WIRES: Unplug the fixture, remove it from the light stand, and lay it tube-side up on the floor. Remove the tubes and the lid that covers the housing containing the wires and ballast. Check for wires that may have worked loose. Remove all the caps that cover the exposed ends of the wires. Make sure the two strands of wires are still tightly twisted together, replace the caps, and give them a twist. Replace the tubes and plug the fixture into an outlet. If the tubes still don't light, it probably means that the ballast has burned out.

Ballasts usually give a warning of their imminent demise by emitting a loud hum, sometimes for weeks in advance.

BALLASTS: Fixtures are available with either conventional magnetic or electronic ballasts. Magnetic ballasts are expensive and may cost as much as the fixtures. But, because of convenience and time, it is usually more practical to replace them. If the old fixtures require a starter, replace with an instant-start ballast. Magnetic ballasts are available at almost all electrical supply stores (electronic replacement ballasts are not available). This is an easy do-it-yourself project for even the non-electrician. The wires are color coded for easy placement. Lay the new ballast by the *unplugged* fixture and study the positioning of the wires as you remove the old ballast. If all else fails, read the directions! If the process is still unclear to you, find an electrician to do the job.

DISPOSAL OF OLD TUBES

Fluorescent tubes contain mercury. Care should be taken not to break a tube. Dispose of burned out tubes as you would hazardous material.

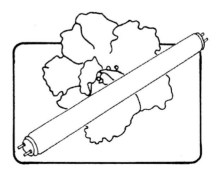

GROWING IN WINDOWS

We have just spent eight pages telling you the ins and outs of growing under artificial lights. But not everyone wants to invest the time, space, or money in a plant stand; much less the people who only really want to enjoy just a few plants. You *can* grow beautiful African violets in windows.

Your window location is going to make a difference. Some homes offer windows on all sides. Some apartments or town-homes have limited window space. Each direction has its own considerations. Keep in mind as each direction is addressed, that it assumes no obstructions. Heavy tree growth, awnings, and neighboring structures also need to be factored in because they may cut down the light significantly.

East: An east-facing window is a wonderful location. The morning sun is gentle and cool.

North: Since a north-facing window is not likely to have any sun, it usually will not have enough bright light for healthy plant growth.

West and South: These directions offer the brightest and hottest light. Be careful! Watch for indications of too much light. Having sheer or opaque curtains or blinds will be a must. Try moving the plants off to the side or on a table that is far enough from the window so the hot sun is not beating directly on them.

No matter which direction your windows face, there is one more big factor. For those who live in the more frigid areas, watch your plants in the winter so they do not get too cold. Any leaves touching the windows will get frostbite. It is not impossible for the whole plant to suffer if the temperature next to your windows is very cold for too many days in a row.

Plants have a natural tendency to lean toward the light source. When growing in windows, the light is always coming from an angle. Each week, when watering your African violets, give them a one-quarter turn. That will help keep them flat and symmetrical.

Temperature

In their native habitat, *Saintpaulia* species grow under a wide range of temperatures. Some species have adapted to warm tropical forests and others thrive in the sometimes frigid conditions of high elevations. However, modern hybrids are subtropical and an ideal temperature range is 75°F during light hours and 65°F during the dark hours. They are among the group of plants that require at least a 10°F drop in nighttime temperature in order to grow and bloom properly.

The ideal temperature range to maintain for show plants is 60° to 80°F. For the casual grower, African violets are quite tolerant of temperatures that are less than ideal. They will survive brief exposures to temperatures as low as 55°F and as high as 90°F. But when these

temperatures are reached, growers must take action to counteract them. Quality will suffer if violets are exposed to these extremes for very long.

Growers who live in areas of extreme weather conditions can duplicate the same conditions as growers who enjoy the conditions of more temperate zones. The difference lies in the expense of artificially creating the most desirable conditions for plants and personal comfort. For areas with seasonal high temperatures, refrigerated air conditioning is the usual cooling method used. This type of air conditioning depletes moisture in the air so that humidity needs to be supplemented. Evaporative water coolers are suited for use only in low-humidity climates, but they do help increase humidity.

It may be necessary to use some form of supplemental heat if the home heating system doesn't keep the plant room temperature at 60°F or more. Heating systems also deplete moisture from the air so that additional humidity must be provided.

HOT DAYS: If the temperature reaches 85°F, turn the lights off for a few hours until the cooler temperatures of the evening prevail. Mist plants every few hours. If you must be away from home during the day, turn the lights off for the entire day. Some growers try to beat the heat by blacking out the room during the heat of the day and burning lights at night when it's cooler. However, this maneuver will be at the expense of plant quality and blossoming because it is difficult to achieve a 10°F drop in temperature during the dark period (daytime). If the room could be kept both cool and dark during the day, then light reversal would work better for combating overly cold night temperatures.

COLD NIGHTS: If temperatures drop below 60°F at night and it isn't practical to run a heater, try tenting the light stands. Plants generate a certain amount of heat during the physiological processes that occur during the dark hours, and so a number of plants grouped together can keep the temperature up by a few degrees if they are contained. Use plastic sheeting and completely drape the plant stands after the lights go off for the night. Pin gaps shut and be sure the plastic extends to the floor. Don't keep the tray matting overly wet during this period, but do keep room humidity up by other means during the light period.

HOT, DRY WINDS: Hot dry winds spell devastation for plants and temporary insanity for people. Most of these types of winds last only a few days and affect both temperature and humidity. To negate their effect shut the house up tight in the morning, add water to the tray matting, run a humidifier, and mist the plants every few hours. Turn off the lights if necessary.

Humidity

It takes the right combination of many factors to grow prime show plants. All of the factors are important but humidity is high on the list. The thick, fleshy leaves of African violets require a high percentage of moisture in the air to keep them at their peak of freshness. If humidity is too low, transpiration (the loss of water through the leaves) takes place more rapidly than the root system can draw water up to the plant tissue. As a result, leaves lose their luster, buds fail to open, and the plants lack general vitality.

A minimum of 50% humidity is desirable, but 60% is even better. You want to stop just short of creating so much humidity that walls and carpeting mildew. Unfortunately, it isn't easy to maintain the proper percentage of humidity in the average home.

Kitchens and bathrooms will periodically have good humidity, but that is not where we usually

grow our plants. Most basements have good humidity, but many homes don't have this convenient space. When plants are grouped together, evaporation from moist soil supplies some humidity but usually not enough.
There is yet another benefit of raising humidity. The people in the household will be more comfortable and will usually have fewer upper

respiratory problems as a result of increased humidity. There are several procedures that may be used singly or in combinations to increase humidity.

Mist plants lightly with a fine-mist sprayer during periods of very low humidity. Use warm or room temperature water and mist during peak temperatures so that the foliage will dry before the lights go out.

The chance of fungus disease increases when foliage stays wet through the dark hours. Line the trays of light stands with matting. Indoor-outdoor carpeting of synthetic pressed-fiber without rubber backing is one type of matting. Acrylic blanket material or commercial matting will also work. The evaporation from the matting will increase the humidity around the plants.

Keep the matting wet but not to the point that pools of water form. Moisture evaporates more quickly from a textured surface than from the smooth surface of a sheet of water.

Keep matting clean by scrubbing it every few months. Acrylic blanket mats and most commercial matting can be washed in the washing machine using detergent and a small amount of bleach

There may be occasional spots of algae or during cold nights a trace of fuzzy mold may form. Use an algaecide in the water or a dilute bleach solution (one teaspoon to one gallon of water) to wet the matting to correct these conditions. Don't splash the bleach solution on the leaves. Also don't use more than the recommended dilution. Fumes from too strong bleach solution can damage foliage.

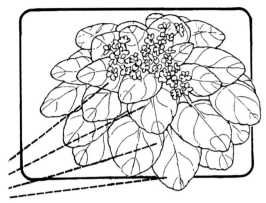

Run a cool-air humidifier in the summer to avoid raising the temperature further. Use a steam humidifier in the winter; the warmer the air the more water vapor it can hold.

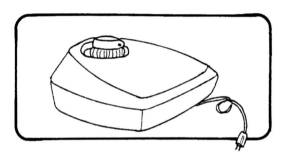

There are a few areas of the country that have the reverse problem of too much humidity. Usually this is a seasonal occurrence. In that case it may be necessary to run a de-humidifier in order to lower humidity and avoid fungus diseases and mildewing of room furnishings.

GAUGES: Place several hygrometers (for measuring relative humidity) and thermometers in various locations around the plant room.

Air Circulation & Ventilation

Fresh, gently moving, warm, humid air – this is a condition we always strive to create for our plants. Air circulation and ventilation are easy to provide, but there are a few precautions to be practiced. It is rarely advisable to have windows open in the plant room. African violets are particularly sensitive to drafts. In addition, thrips and aphids from an outside garden can easily come through screening. Introduce fresh air daily from a room adjacent to the plant room. Adequate air movement is usually generated by the comings and goings of people. However, if there is little air movement, particularly during warm weather, a small fan operating during light hours is helpful. It can be plugged into the timer unit. The fan should not blow directly on the plants.

THE RIGHT ENVIRONMENT

LIGHT:
- Light fixtures should be 8" to 10" above foliage for mature standards; 6" to 8" for miniatures and semiminiatures.

- Average light hours from 8 to 10 hours; increase when getting ready for show. Fluorescent lights should be on a timer.

TEMPERATURE:
- Ideal temperature range is from 60° to 80°F.

- If you are comfortable, your violets will be happy.

HUMIDITY:
- Keep humidity between 50% and 60%.

AIR CIRCULATION:
- Circulate air with fans; plant foliage should not touch.

pH: a Vital Factor

New growers may become discouraged by all the information they are trying to absorb at once. So, when an intangible like pH comes up, it seems like the last straw. Don't panic; understanding the basic function of pH eliminates the mystery.

Puissance de hydrogen (hydrogen-ion concentration), or pH, is the expression of the relative level of acidity or alkalinity of any substance. A neutral pH is expressed as 7.0. Above 7.0 is alkaline and below 7.0 is acidic. Each full point, either up or down, is either 10 times more acidic or more alkaline.

By using a good quality potting mix and repotting regularly, the casual grower need not be too concerned about pH if the water has a neutral or only slightly alkaline pH, since the fertilizers added to it are slightly acidic.

African violets grow and bloom best in a pH range of 6.2 to 6.9. The soilless potting mix that most growers use for African violets (usually a mixture of perlite, vermiculite, and Canadian peat moss), if properly amended with dolomite lime, should be slightly acidic and measure 6.5 to 6.7 pH. The pH of water varies a great deal depending on its source and treatment and must be considered along with the fertilizer and potting mix .

pH has everything to do with nutrients. When the pH of the potting mix, fertilizer, and water combination is below or above the 6.2 to 6.9 pH range, the major nutrient elements (macronutrients), nitrogen, potassium, and especially phosphorus are "locked-up" and not available to the plant. If phosphorus is unavailable to the plant, the micronutrients, such as boron, manganese, copper, iron, molybdenum, and zinc, may be released in amounts toxic to the plant. This accumulation of excessive levels of these trace elements builds up in the tissues of the plant over time. Unfortunately, visual identification of this problem, called *micronutrient toxicity*, is difficult to detect, and irreversible damage may occur before symptoms are apparent.

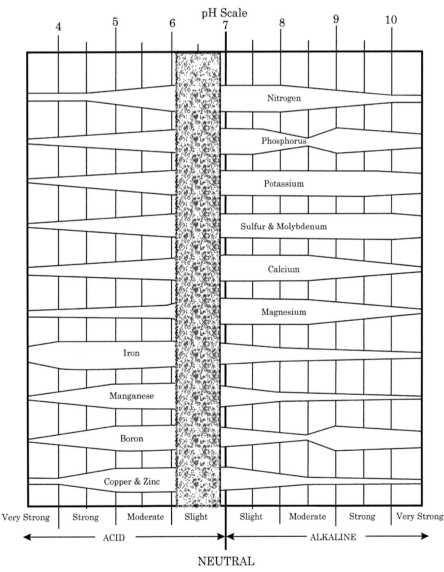

The shaded area indicates the ideal pH range for African violets.

Symptoms of micronutrient toxicity include: slow, stunted growth; light green to yellowish green foliage; dark, brittle older foliage; fewer blossoms that are small and may not open or are off-color; small, tight, crisp center leaf growth; extensive suckering; and, culture break between larger older leaves and new growth, depending on when the toxic effects began in the growth cycle of the plant. Leaf deformity is most evident in older, lower leaves, but recently matured leaves will twist and curl and eventually the new center leaves will be twisted and deformed.

The plants don't "die" and the roots look normal, but eventually, the centers will deteriorate and what's left isn't pretty! Many plants have gone to make compost before they get this bad. Unfortunately the tissues in the leaves will be damaged, and while they may propagate with apparently healthy plantlets, the new plantlets will eventually develop symptoms. So you should throw out the damaged plants, take no leaves, and learn to check the potting mix and water pH (See pH Testing, p. 43).

Over a period of time, the peat moss in potting mix breaks down and becomes more acidic. This is a slow process and with the frequent repotting practiced by show growers, this is usually not a problem if the pH of the potting mix is within range when repotted. After a plant has been potted up it makes no sense to pour vinegar or other acidic solution through the soil to correct an alkaline condition when you can start out with the proper pH in the first place. Also a calcium or lime drench is only a temporary solution to correct a too-acid potting mix. pH testing should be a part of every serious African violet grower's regimen (See Methods of Testing pH, p. 44).

---

pH Summary

- African violets grow and bloom best in a pH range of 6.2 to 6.9.

- If correct pH is not maintained, a plant can virtually "starve" because of it's inability to absorb nutrients it needs.

- All essential nutrient elements including micronutrients are available to the plants when the soil/water/fertilizer pH is in the 6.2 to 6.9 pH range.

- When the pH is below 6.0 or above 7.0, phosphorus becomes "locked-up" and unavailable, which allows micronutrients to become toxic to African violets.

- Test the pH of the potting mix before using it whether you mix it yourself or you use a commercial mix. Potting mix pH should measure between 6.5 and 6.7.

- Test the pH of potting mix with the fertilizer water you use for your plants; most fertilizers are acidic.

- The pH of water varies with its source and treatment. Water pH contributes to the total pH in the plant's root zone.

- Repot to avoid decomposition of peat, which becomes more acidic over time.
  - Repot standards every four to six months.
  - Repot miniatures and semiminiatures every two to three months.

Potting Mix

There are good potting mixes and bad potting mixes but there are too many factors involved to label any one mix as perfect or "magic." Most of today's growers use a recipe that involves Canadian peat moss, vermiculite, and perlite, commonly referred to as "soilless" mix. Many of them will add things that they hope will be the "magic bullet."

Few growers now include natural soil in potting mixes. Garden soil has too many drawbacks for delicate, fibrous-rooted plants such as African violets because it compacts rapidly, has poor aeration, and must be pasteurized before use.

Some commercial mixes are quite satisfactory, particularly the ones that are packaged regionally because the pH is often adjusted to accommodate the pH of the water supply in the area. Unfortunately, some potting mixes labeled for African violets may contain fertilizers and the pH may vary considerably. Now and then manufacturers substitute cheaper, less desirable materials to avoid raising the price of the mix.

There are advantages to mixing your own: the manufacturer won't go out of business, the grower has quality control, the mix is always on hand, and the savings are considerable. There are, however, disadvantages to mixing your own. Ingredients can be hard to find, there may be differences in their quality, and storage space is needed for excess ingredients

POTTING MIX INGREDIENTS

If you mix your own, it is less expensive to buy large quantities of the ingredients. All three components of the mix can be found where horticulture supplies are sold. Some growers prefer coarser versions of perlite (sponge rock) and vermiculite, which can be ordered from Internet sources.

PEAT MOSS is a fluffy, acidic, organic material that resists compaction. Once dampened, it

has great water and nutrient-holding capacity; however, it has few nutrients. *Peat moss can measure as low as 3.5 to 5.5 pH* and tends to become more acidic as it decomposes. Michigan and Colorado peat are available, but the quality is inferior to Canadian peat. Peat can vary in pH and quality from source to source.

A 2-1/2 cubic foot bale of Canadian milled sphagnum peat moss will make several batches of potting mix.

PERLITE provides aeration in a potting mix and has some water-holding capacity. It resists compaction and keeps the mix loose and well aerated, promoting good drainage and allowing oxygen to flow to roots. It is an expanded volcanic material that is virtually chemically inert with fluorides present only in trace amounts. The pH is neutral, approximately 7.0.

VERMICULITE has water- and nutrient-holding capacity and acts as a buffering agent to slow changes in pH. It is chemically active and contains small amounts of magnesium, aluminum, and silica, and traces of potassium and calcium. The pH is generally thought to be neutral, but it may vary from source to source. According to the Vermiculite Association, horticultural vermiculite has a pH range of 6.0 to 9.5.

Construction-grade vermiculite is used for making insulation. This kind of vermiculite is to be avoided because of possible additives that may be toxic to plants.

DOLOMITE LIME is calcium magnesium carbonate with a pH of 8.8. It is used to correct the acidity of peat. Dolomite lime is sold as a powdered mixture like flour, or as a mixed grind (different size particles). The finer the grind, the more quickly it reacts to reduce acidity in the potting mix.

Do not use hydrated lime; it is very fast acting and will burn the roots.

OPTIONAL INGREDIENTS

Charcoal retains (or binds up) organic by-products (gases from decomposing matter) from the mix, keeping the mix "sweet." With the frequent potting required to grow show plants, charcoal is not an essential ingredient in potting mix. Use only horticultural or aquarium grade charcoal.

Superphosphate is a slow-release form of phosphorus–one of the primary elements that is difficult for plants to assimilate from liquid fertilizer. Superphosphate is a natural material containing many elements including sulfur, calcium, iron, and magnesium. This is an optional ingredient in many potting mix recipes.

If you buy it, look for 0-20-0 (meaning 0% nitrogen, 20% phosphorus, 0% potassium). Superphosphate comes in a granular form. To properly distribute a small amount throughout the mix, it should be ground into a finer form.

Styrofoam pellets are used in some potting mixes in place of perlite. Styrofoam is light and provides some aeration to the soil, but it does not have the water-holding properties of perlite.

Lava rock is added to the potting mix (one cup to one gallon of mix) by growers who report positive results, especially with variegates. It is an inert substance that does not change the pH. It is unclear how it affects plants; it may be a catalyst in the assimilation of nutrients. It provides aeration to the root zone. Buy horticulture grade lava rock chips (about the size of perlite) available at garden supply centers.

Trace minerals do not need to be added to potting mix. Trace minerals are already present in some of the potting-mix ingredients, local water supplies, and many fertilizers. An excess of trace minerals can be harmful to plants.

EQUIPMENT

Thirty-gallon plastic containers with tight fitting lids are ideal for storing perlite, vermiculite and peat moss. These ingredients may be kept in the original bags, but it isn't recommended for long-term storage because of leakage from punctures or tears. This size container is also useful for mixing and storing large batches of mix. Large plastic pails with tight-fitting lids or clamp-on lids are useful for storing the mix; the tight lids keep the mixture moist.

You will also need cups or containers for measuring ingredients. One- or two-quart measuring containers and gallon pails may be items you have around the house, such as one-quart yogurt containers or coffee cans. Other useful items are a large, sturdy long-handled spoon (or disposable plastic gloves so you can mix with your hands); disposable molded painter's mask; and wetting agent, sometimes referred to as a "surfactant."

RECIPES

Soilless potting mix recipes include peat, perlite, and vermiculite plus optional ingredients such as charcoal. Cornell University published a soilless potting mix recipe, which many growers adjust to their growing conditions. The *Cornell recipe*: one or two parts peat, one part perlite, and one part vermiculite with dolomite lime added to adjust the pH. Charcoal is optional. This recipe works well for wick watering, which requires a light, well-drained mix.

Many growers use commercial mixes and amend them to meet their needs. There are no standards for commercial potting mixes. Read the labels and avoid mixes with fertilizer added. Check with local greenhouses and nurseries; many use commercial soilless mixes. Be sure to ask about additional ingredients.

Over the sixty years of the *African Violet Magazine,* a large number of potting mix recipes have been included in articles describing a wide variety of formulas and ingredients.

The following recipe was formulated for the Texas-Style potting method, but it is also suitable for other growing methods:

> 5 quarts dry peat moss (fluffed)
> 4 quarts #2 perlite
> 3 quarts vermiculite
> 1 cup charcoal (optional)
> 1 tablespoon Superphosphate 0-20-0
> Dolomite lime to adjust the pH

MIXING

For proper distribution of ingredients, mix only one batch at a time. Always wear a mask when measuring and stirring the mix; some of the ingredients are powdery and inhaling the dust may cause health problems.

1. Measure the peat moss into a large plastic tub and sift through it with your hand. Crumble away the lumps, discarding twigs and other debris.

   Add one quart of hot water. Stir, mix, and knead until every particle of peat moss is completely moistened. To facilitate the wetting of the peat, five drops of wetting agent may be added to each quart of water.

2. Add the dolomite lime and Superphosphate. Start by adding one-tablespoon dolomite to two quarts of *moistened* peat. Mix thoroughly until they are evenly distributed. Dissemination is important since these two ingredients are in small proportion to the volume of the other ingredients. It is also important that the mix be damp. The chemical particles will cling to a damp mix rather than sifting back to the bottom during the mixing process.

   Dolomite lime is added to raise the pH of the mix to between 6.5 and 6.7. The coarseness (or fineness) of the grind is a determining factor in how much to add; however, a pH test is the only way to know how much dolomite to add.

3. Add the perlite, vermiculite, and charcoal. Toss gently until evenly distributed. Add another 1/2 quart of water and mix again. The mix should be fluffy and free pouring, not wet and soggy. Press a handful into a ball; it should be moist enough to just barely hold its shape. Once you start potting you will realize the importance of the proper moistness of the potting mix.

4. Store the *moistened* mix for two weeks before testing. Repeat the pH test each time a new batch is mixed.

pH TESTING

Getting an accurate pH reading is the most frustrating part of making your own mix, but it can make all the difference in the quality of the mix and the health of the plants.

Two basic products used for determining pH of a potting mix are pH test strips and electronic pH testers (pens). The pH test strips can be purchased where aquarium or pool and spa supplies are sold. Testing with pH test strips will give adequate information to determine the pH of mixes. *Follow the instructions on the pH test strip package carefully.* Some pH strips must be left in the water for fifteen seconds or more and then compared to the color chart on the package; others must be dipped into the water, removed and read immediately. Using aquarium or pool pH testing kits with the *pour-through pH method*, it is possible to get measurements that are accurate enough to tell if your mix is in the approximate 6.5 to 6.7 range.

Soil test probes, sold at garden supply centers, are designed for compact garden soil and do not work in loose potting mix. For more accurate testing, hand-held electronic pH testers (pens) are available. Most are sold by scientific equipment supply sources. An electronic pH pen would be a reasonable investment for the show grower who has a large collection of plants, whether using commercial or home made potting mix.

Private testing laboratories will check the pH of soil and water, but this is expensive and will need to be repeated each time a new batch is mixed.

Regardless of the type of test equipment used, several samples should be tested and compared. If repeat tests agree that the pH is 6.5 to 6.7, you may then breathe a sigh of relief and start using your mix. But if the mix is too acid or too alkaline, the amount of dolomite lime will have to be adjusted and the tests repeated. If the pH is too acid, add dolomite lime in increments of 1/2 teaspoon per gallon of mix, retesting each time. If the pH is too alkaline, make a new batch of mix, reduce the amount of dolomite lime and add by 1/2 teaspoon increments until the desired pH is obtained; or, add a known quantity of peat to the mix, add water, let stand and re-test.

METHODS OF TESTING pH

There are two methods of doing pH tests – "pour-through" and "slurry" (soil solution). The "pour-through" method measures the pH of the water that has been poured through a potted plant or container of soil mix. The pH test strips are adequate for this method. An electronic testing pen is ideal for the slurry test.

If you want to know the pH of the mix, use distilled water; however, since water and fertilizer contribute to the total pH of the mix surrounding the plants' roots it is important to use the fertilizer water to moisten the mix and use in testing.

Follow the steps using one of the methods outlined below to measure the pH of the water, potting mix, and/or combined fertilizer water and potting mix:

Pour-Through pH Test

To check the pH of the soilless mix:

1. Fill a 3" or 4" pot with moistened potting mix; add distilled water to saturate the mix to the capacity of water it will hold. Some will leach out into a saucer. Let the moistened mix sit for 30 minutes to 2 hours.

2. Drain off the excess water and discard.

3. Place the container in a shallow saucer.

4. Pour distilled water slowly over the surface of the soil until it drains into the saucer.

5. Test the leached water with pH test strips or electronic testing pen. Read and record the results. Record the formula or source of the mix and date of the test.

To check the pH of soil, water and fertilizer:

Repeat the test using the fertilizer water you use with your violets; record the pH and date of test.

To check the pH of the mix in a potted plant:

Be sure that it has been watered several days ahead of the test and is moist but not saturated. Pour enough distilled water to run through, collecting and testing what flows out.

Slurry Test

1. Mix 1 part potting mix to 1 part distilled water in a small container; mix vigorously.

2. Allow the mixture to stand approximately 30 minutes then stir well.

3. It is not necessary to strain the solution before testing with an electronic pH tester.

   To test with a pH strip, strain the solution through a fine mesh or cheesecloth.

4. Repeat the test using fertilizer water.

PASTEURIZING

Pasteurization of potting mix was essential when leaf mold, compost, or garden soil were used, but they are not recommended in modern day potting mix for African violets. If you do choose to pasteurize, here's how to proceed.

PASTEURIZING IN OVEN: Place dampened peat moss in a large, baked enamel canning kettle. Tightly seal the top with heavy-duty aluminum foil and insert a meat thermometer through the foil. Indent the center of the foil so the tip of the thermometer reaches the center of the mix. Bake at 350° for approximately 2-3 hours. The temperature must rise to 180°F and be maintained for 30 minutes. It is not possible to determine exactly how long it will take to complete the process

After pasteurizing, loosen the foil (be careful of steam), and stir the peat moss until it is cool enough to store. Since beneficial microorganisms have been temporarily suppressed, care must be taken to avoid contamination.

PASTEURIZING IN MICROWAVE: A small amount of potting mix may be pasteurized in a microwave oven. Place the moist mix in a microwaveable bowl, cover with plastic wrap, and microwave on high for eight to ten minutes, stirring several times; check the temperature with a meat thermometer.

Fertilizing

There are no days off or vacations for show plants. They are constantly under artificial light so that the leaf size and the quality of symmetry never lag. At least once a year, these plants are required to go into peak bloom for show exhibition. Plants will meet these high standards if they are fed properly. The fertilizing program must be as steady as the programs for light, water, and grooming.

FERTILIZER: An enriching material used in soil (or soilless potting mix) to increase its productivity. Thirteen elements are required for proper plant growth.

MAJOR ELEMENTS: Nitrogen, phosphorus, and potassium.

SECONDARY ELEMENTS: Sulfur, calcium, and magnesium.

TRACE ELEMENTS: Zinc, copper, chlorine, manganese, iron, boron, and molybdenum.

(FREE ELEMENTS of carbon, hydrogen, and oxygen are supplied by air and water.)

A well-balanced diet is essential, so a balanced fertilizer is used. This is a fertilizer that contains the three MAJOR ELEMENTS (not necessarily in equal proportions). SECONDARY ELEMENTS are supplied in sufficient quantities by some of the ingredients of the potting mix. TRACE ELEMENTS are present in community water supplies (sometimes in overabundant amounts) and are contained, but sometimes unlisted, in many fertilizers. They are not always included on the label because they may vary slightly and, therefore, cannot be legally certified.

Fertilizer fortified with the trace elements of zinc and iron (chelated) work well for all-green foliaged plants, but variegated varieties loose their variegation. Also, multi-colored and edged blossoms may revert to solid color.

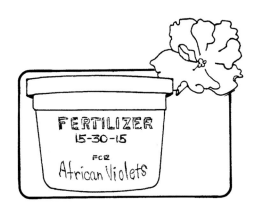

FERTILIZER LABELS: To provide the right kind of food, the grower needs to understand fertilizer labels. Labels of balanced fertilizers list the percentage of the three major elements. The fine print lists the percentage of the elements by name. Prominently displayed in bolder print, the information is typically given in the form of three numbers: 20-20-20, 15-30-15, 12-36-14, and so on. The first number represents the percentage of nitrogen (N), the second number the percentage of phosphorus (P), and the third number the percentage of potassium (K).

NITROGEN develops maximum color of foliage, promotes leaf and petiole growth, improves the quality of plant tissue, influences rapid growth, and increases the protein content of plants.

PHOSPHORUS stimulates early root formation and growth, gives a vigorous start to plants, hastens maturity and stimulates formation of blossoms.

POTASSIUM imparts vigor and resistance to disease, improves reproductive quality, and is essential to formation and transfer of starches and sugars to the plant system.

In brief: Nitrogen for foliage, phosphorus for blossoms, and potassium for general health.

ORGANIC & INORGANIC FERTILIZERS: Most indoor gardeners prefer to use inorganic fertilizers. These are nutrients manufactured from chemical components. Organic fertilizers are those derived from natural matter such as fish or animal sources. Even though manufacturers have removed much of the offensive odor from these fertilizers, they leave a residue in the saucers that will eventually smell as it decomposes.

Organic fertilizers are not used with bottom watering procedures (Texas-Style, matting, or wicking) because they plug up capillaries. This slows or stops the process of capillary attraction.

The hobbyist grower will want to look for certain requirements when choosing fertilizers:

1. The percentages of the three major elements (NPK) should add up to approximately 60% (the remaining percentage is made up of inert ingredients and trace elements).

2. The type of fertilizer is soluble (often called "wettable powder"). This type is meant to be used in water, not as an additive to soil mixes.

Percentages of the major elements that add up to less (14-12-14 = 40%) or more (7-50-17 = 70%) than 60% (20-20-20) work equally well. The disadvantage is that in some cases a complicated mathematical formula would have to be applied in order to arrive at the amount required for a dilute solution to be used in a constant feed program. When using different fertilizers, the grower would perhaps have to remember to use a third of a teaspoon of one kind and half a teaspoon of another. So make it easy for yourself by using only those fertilizers that add up to approximately 60%. Many of the major brands have this percentage.

Fertilizers are produced from several different sources. Many of the less expensive fertilizers use urea, ammonium phosphate, and/or ammoniacal nitrogen as the source of nitrogen. Fertilizers that use a nitrate base are more expensive but do not pose the problems caused by urea-based fertilizers. Fertilizers that use a nitrate base are recommended for African violets. Read the labels and select a fertilizer with little or no urea or ammonia based ingredients.

CONSTANT FEED & DILUTE FERTILIZER SOLUTIONS

CONSTANT FEED: Using a dilute fertilizer solution each time plants are watered.

DILUTE SOLUTION: In horticultural language this refers to a fertilizer solution diluted to proportions usually less than the recommended amount. It is essential in a steady, controlled program.

AMOUNT TO USE: The proper dilution for a 60% fertilizer is 1/4 teaspoon to a gallon of water. This solution can be mixed and stored; there is no deterioration. Fertilizers have an indefinite shelf life and do not lose their effectiveness even though they may cake or become semi-liquefied as they absorb moisture.

SUPERTHRIVE®: Add one drop to each gallon of dilute fertilizer solution as a boost to plant growth.

PLAIN FOLIAGE VARIETIES: Use a balanced fertilizer (20-20-20) for most of the year. This encourages general growth and leaf size during the period plants are being trained for symmetry. Many growers use 15-30-15, or a similar formula with a higher percentage of phosphorus, throughout the year to promote root development and blooming.

FERTILIZING VARIEGATED FOLIAGE VARIETIES: Use a lower-nitrogen content fertilizer. This encourages the coloration of the variegation and discourages an undesirable amount of green from developing. Use 15-30-15, 12-36-14 or a similar formula. The continuous use of a formula containing less than 10% nitrogen is not recommended for show plants where the formation of foliage and leaf size is a primary factor.

BLOOM BOOSTERS: To bring plants into full bloom for a show, a special schedule using a low-nitrogen, high-phosphorus "bloom booster" fertilizer is put into effect. Bloom boosters have numbers like 5-50-17. Note that this is a 70% NPK fertilizer with very low nitrogen.

FOLIAR FEEDING

Except as a growth and blossom booster before a show, African violets do not need a steady diet of foliar feeding. The benefit of foliar feeding African violets has not been supported by scientific study. The extra nutrients can create an excess of fertilizer that causes leaf and crown burn, tight centers, and loss of variegation. Many growers do not foliar feed their show plants; others foliar feed according to the pre-show calendar.

Plants absorb only a small percentage of organic fertilizers, so they are relatively ineffectual for foliar feeding. Plants absorb more nutrients when foliar fed with an inorganic fertilizer; however, not all fertilizers are suitable for foliar feeding. Read the labels.

If you choose to foliar feed, mix the proper amount of fertilizer (check the label) with warm or room temperature water. Use distilled or reverse osmosis water; excess mineral content in water can spot foliage. It is helpful to add a few drops of a wetting agent (or two or three drops of mild dish detergent) to the fertilizer solution so it won't bead on the foliage. Spray during the light period when the temperature is between 75°F and 80°F (foliage should be dry before the lights go off) and spray the bottom side of leaves where most of the *stomata* (cells allow gases and vapors to pass into and out of the leaf) are located. After spraying, pat up excess solution in the crown of the plants with a tissue or soft sponge.

FOLIAR FEEDING VARIEGATES: Variegated plants may loose their variegation with foliar feeding. An exception is when variegated plantlets show almost no green; the extra nitrogen from foliar feeding may help them green-up. Some growers report that they have no problems when foliar feeding variegated varieties.

CAUTION: *Always test on a few plants well in advance of a show before spraying your entire collection.*

LEACHING

Leaching is the flushing away of accumulated fertilizer salts by pouring a quantity of plain water through the soil of a potted plant. Because of the constant replacement of old soil by frequent re-potting, leaching is not a necessary standard practice for show-plant growers. However, leaching every three or four weeks cannot hurt and can be beneficial to all plants. Time may be a big factor to many growers.

There will be an occasional problem of burned centers with some more-sensitive varieties even though they are on the same fertilizing program as the rest of the collection. If they are good show quality specimens, they can be given special treatment by leaching once a month or so. For supersensitive varieties, use a more diluted solution of fertilizer (1/8-teaspoon to a gallon of water). When leaching, use about two cups of plain water for 4" and 5" pots and up to one quart of water for 6" and 8" pots.

Casual growers who repot less frequently than show-growers should leach about every two months as a standard practice.

FERTILIZING TIPS

- African violets are heavy feeders and they will deplete normal potting soil relatively quickly. Soilless mixes require constant fertilizer for optimum growth and blooming. Regularly fertilize with 1/4 tsp. fertilizer per gallon of water.

- Temperature and amount of light affect the amount of fertilizer the plants can use. With cooler temperatures and less light (window grown plants in winter), cut to 1/8 tsp. per gallon and eliminate fertilizer every other watering until growing conditions improve.

- Never try a new fertilizer regiment on more than a few plants; never your whole collection until you know it works for you.

- Never fertilize a wilted or dry plant; fertilizer can burn the tiny feeder roots that are already under stress from lack of water or repotting.

- Chemical reactions in your plants depend on soil, water, light, and fertilizer; be aware that these factors work together for optimum nutrition for your plants.

- African violets will only use what they need from the fertilizer and any excess is left to build up in the soil. Repot regularly or leach with plain water every two months.

- Rotation of fertilizers is recommended for African Violets to provide a "balanced diet" for the plants. Some brands of fertilizers contain more of the micronutrients than others and also use different percentages of both the macro- and micronutrients.

- Read the ingredient labels on the fertilizer container. Avoid fertilizers with high urea content.

Water Quality

Water! Water everywhere! But is it fit for African violets? Not for the most part it seems. Many community water supplies have a high percentage of parts per million (ppm) dissolved solids. Some communities have added fluorides to the water (great for teeth, not so great for plants). Most municipal water contains chlorine, which will dissipate in a few hours in an open container; however, over 20 percent of all municipal water is now treated with chloramines, which does not dissipate and is detrimental to African violets. Rainwater the world over has become increasingly acidic. Well-water sometimes contains excessive amounts of minerals such as iron. And many homes have a water-softening unit, which raises the saline content of the water. Unless you have access to pure natural spring water, you may want to look for an alternative to the water that comes from your tap.

The first step is to determine just what the quality of the water is that is being piped into your home. If it has been artificially softened, you will want to find another source of water for your plants. If it is from your own private well, have it analyzed. If it comes from a community water supply, you can get an idea of its quality by calling the local water company, which can give you the figures from the most recent analysis report.

When having water tested there are three major components of water quality to consider. You will want to know the Total Dissolved Solids (TDS), the Electrical Conductivity (EC), and the pH of the water. If your water source is a municipal water supply, you will want to find out what chemical treatments have been added.

TOTAL DISSOLVED SOLIDS (TDS) are the total amount of mobile charged ions, including minerals, salts or metals dissolved in a given volume of water and is expressed in parts per million (ppm). TDS include anything present other than the pure water molecules and

suspended solids. Ideal drinking water, reverse osmosis, deionized and distilled water have from 0 to 49 ppm total dissolved solids; carbon filtered water will have from 50 to 99 ppm; hard water is from 100-199 ppm; average tap water measures from 200-399 ppm. If the ppm total dissolved solids (TDS) are over 400 you should find another source of water.

Most of us recognize the "hardness" of our water when we use soap or shampoo. A laboratory test for alkalinity (hardness) of water is expressed as milligrams calcium carbonate per liter (mg/L). The best range for plants is about 80 to 100 mg/L expressed as calcium carbonate. This measure is a conversion of the test for electrical conductivity.

ELECTRICAL CONDUCTIVITY (EC) is directly related to the concentration of dissolved ionized solids in the water; it is a measure of a material's ability to conduct an electric current, which can be measured using a conventional conductivity meter. Most growers will not invest in such a meter; however, a water-testing laboratory may provide a reading in microsiemens (uS/cm) per liter. You should know that the recommended EC for African violets is between 260 and 750 uS/cm (just remember the numbers). High mineral content in the water and fertilizer salt build-up in the soil will increase the EC.

Well water and city water vary and the only way to know is to have the water tested. Tests have shown that electrical conductivity varies a great deal with different water sources.

pH is the measure of the acidity or alkalinity of water. This was discussed in the section on pH. (See pH: A Vital Factor.) Ideally, the pH of the potting mix is adjusted to accommodate the fertilizer water; however, numerous growers use products to adjust the pH of the water. If the alkalinity of the water is between 80 and 100 mg/L expressed as calcium carbonate, use it without adjusting the pH.

Products sold for hydroponics and aquarium use to raise or lower pH are often highly concentrated and care must be taken with their use. Vinegar will act as a pH down product because of the acetic acid it contains; however, it is a weak organic acid and will decompose in the soil rather quickly. Water standing over a period of time will pick up dissolved carbon dioxide and will become slightly acidic. Many fertilizers will increase the pH in the soil. The only way to be sure about the pH is to test the water and the potting mix.

There are other factors in water analysis to be considered. In some areas of the country, sodium chloride and boron concentrations are high and these figures can be difficult for the layman to interpret. The surest way to get the right information is to call the county or state agricultural extension office in your area or contact a private water-testing laboratory. They have experts who have analyzed local water and can advise you about the water quality in your area.

MUNICIPAL WATER varies from city to city depending on the source–deep wells, reservoirs, rivers–and on the treatment used to make the water safe for drinking. Chlorine has long been used to treat city water. Growers know that chlorine dissipates if the water is left to sit at room temperature for a few hours. More recently, *chloramines* are being used by up to one-quarter of all municipal treatment plants to kill microorganisms in the water and make it safe for drinking.

Chloramines release chlorine and ammonia into water over time. Chloramines are toxic to fish, amphibians and reptiles; small amounts may not harm plants but they will become toxic over time. Symptoms of toxicity are: leaves wilt and turn to jelly, edges appear brown in color (necrosis), and failure to bloom.

Chloramines are not removed from water by boiling or sitting a few days and reverse osmosis units will not remove the chloramines unless they have aquarium type charcoal filtration. Aquarium products will remove the chloramines, but read the labels; *they should remove both the chlorine and ammonia.*

REVERSE-OSMOSIS (RO) SYSTEMS can be purchased or rented and installed under the kitchen sink. They remove 70% to 85% (depending on the age of the filter) of harmful impurities and the pH of reverse osmosis water is usually 7.0 to 7.3 pH. To a certain extent, the quality of reverse osmosis water is dependent upon the quality of the water going into the system.

One of the benefits of reverse osmosis water, which is often first run through a water-softening unit to remove most of the dissolved solids, is the lack of mineral build-up on reservoir trays. The downside is that the electrical conductivity of RO water is about 30; below that recommended for African violets. It may be beneficial to mix RO water with another water source to bring the EC up to the recommended level.

Reverse osmosis units come in several sizes, but for watering plants and people, the three-gallon size is the most practical in space requirements and volume. Up to four or five gallons may be drawn from this size in a 12-hour period.

DISTILLING UNITS are on the market; they come in all sizes. However, distilled water is completely lacking in minerals. Plants need a certain amount of minerals in the water, and so, depending on the quality of the local water, about one part tap water should be added to each three parts distilled water.

BOTTLED SPRING WATER is a good source of quality water, but using it depends on your budget and your energy.

Watering Methods

Several methods of watering are used for African violets: top, bottom, wick, and mat. Self-watering pots and the Texas-style potting method use bottom-watering techniques. Some of the newer self-watering pots function on the same principle as wicking reservoirs.

Texas-style potting introduced the use of a bottom layer of perlite in the pot. A modified method, which uses the perlite layer in the bottom of the pot plus wicking or matting, is widely used and has replaced the true Texas-style in popularity. With a perlite layer the roots have breathing space even if the grower is somewhat heavy-handed with the water. On the other hand, the perlite layer retains enough moisture to maintain the roots if too little water is given.

Watering is one of the most difficult skills to learn in growing African violets. With the conventional method of top watering, it often takes a beginning grower many years to learn how to water properly. Drowning is the most common method of killing violets. After many warnings from veteran growers, the beginner would be so afraid of over-watering that the root ball would rattle around dry in the pot.

The best way of developing watering skills is by learning to judge the moisture content of a pot by feeling the top of the soil. The experienced grower can also tell from the heft of the pot how much moisture remains. For example, a pot that still feels heavy at the end of the watering interval means that one of four conditions exist:

1. The plant has been recently potted so that the root system is not yet mature enough to use up all the water.

2. A particular variety has a genetically sparse or weak root system so that water is not being used to the fullest extent. (If this is the case, do not pot these varieties beyond a 4" or 5" pot.)

3. A particular variety has an exceptionally dense, heavy root system.

4. A pest or pathogen has damaged the roots to the extent that the plant no longer has a full complement of healthy roots to take up the water.

Care must be taken to assure that violets are not over-watered because this can also block airflow to the root system.

Respiration takes place in two areas of a plant: foliage and root tips. It is essential to the health of plants that a free flow of air is available to both of these areas. The leaves should be kept free of dust and dirt, and the roots should have ample breathing space; but the real magic takes place in the perlite layer where the following two actions take place:

1. *Air spaces in the perlite layer allow the free exchange of gases at the root tips.* Like humans, plants have to breathe to live. We take in oxygen and give off carbon dioxide; but plants do just the opposite–they take in carbon dioxide and give off oxygen. This transfer is called the "gas exchange." Whether in plants or animals, the gas exchange can take place only in air. Air spaces are present in a porous potting mix to a more restricted degree. By providing the root system with additional air space in the perlite layer, plant growth is given a big boost.

2. *Roots have free access to moisture and nutrients in the perlite layer.* Even under optimum conditions, getting the proper amount of water and nourishment is a traumatic experience for the roots of container-grown plants. The roots are in competition with the soil for water, which, to some degree, is made physically unavailable by absorption into the peat moss.

With the exception of top watering, *capillary action* takes place to get water into the root zone. This process takes place even if a perlite layer is not used.

The nutrient solution is in the saucer or reservoir and by wicking is drawn up to the root system by capillary action. The air spaces between particles, including the perlite layer or particles in the potting mix, form a myriad of little "tubes" or capillaries. Wicking material acts as capillaries taking the water up into the potting mix according to the needs of the plant.

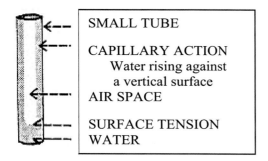

SMALL TUBE

CAPILLARY ACTION
    Water rising against
    a vertical surface
AIR SPACE

SURFACE TENSION
WATER

A *capillary* is defined as having a very small internal diameter, as a tube. *Capillary action* (or attraction) is the force that causes a liquid to rise against a vertical surface such as water in a small glass vial. The molecules in water create tension, such as water beading on a smooth surface. It is this *surface tension* that starts the action of capillary attraction.

Many growers individually water all of their show plants because it allows them to keep a close eye on them and they groom their plants each time they water. Growers who have hundreds of plants (and there are a lot of them out there!) find that giving individual attention to each plant is far too time-consuming and tedious. Growers with large collections find continuous watering methods convenient and time saving.

TOP WATERING

Growers with a small number of plants may find it convenient to top-water individual plants on an as needed basis. Water is slowly poured into the top of the pot until water drains out of the drainage holes. The pot is on a saucer to collect the excess water, which must be emptied within thirty minutes or so. Avoid getting water in the center of the plant. If it does, gently dab it out with a tissue or soft sponge. Water from the side, under the leaves; a watering can with a long spout works well for top watering.

BOTTOM WATERING

Each plant is individually watered by adding water to a saucer or tray. Water depths are measured with the pots remaining in the saucers or trays. Most of the water will be taken up (by capillary action) by the end of the day. If there is still water in the saucer or tray in an hour or so, pour it out and allow the pot to drain off any excess water. As you gain experience, you will soon be able to add just the right amount of water. No need to use a ruler; your best guess will be close enough. Between watering intervals the soil should range from wet to barely moist, but the top of the soil should not be allowed to dry out completely.

2-1/2" pots: Cafeteria-style trays are convenient to use. Add about 1/4" of water to the trays every three or four days. The depth will vary depending on how many pots are on the tray.

4", 5", 6", 7", and 8" pots: Depending on weather conditions, water about every four to five days for 4" and 5" pots and every five to six days for 6", 7", and 8" pots. On the scheduled watering day, if the soil still feels quite moist (usually the condition of recently potted plants), add 1/4" of water to the saucer. If the soil feels barely moist (usually the condition of established plants), add 3/8" to 1/2" of water.

Caution: Don't leave water in the saucers for longer than a few hours; plants will usually take all the water the mix will hold within an hour.

WICK WATERING

Many growers use a wick-watering system for their African violets. This is referred to as "constant" or "continuous" watering since water is always available to the plants. Wick watering works on the same principle as an oil lamp (another example of capillary action). Water is kept in a reservoir and is soaked up by a wick that leads into the soil around the roots of the violet. This allows growers even longer intervals between watering, depending on the size of the reservoir.

There are two popular methods of wick watering: individual reservoirs for single plants, and trays fitted with "egg-crating" (sometimes referred to as humidity grids) to accommodate a large number of plants. Nylon cord and acrylic yarn make good wicks because these synthetic materials will not deteriorate over time but natural fibers such as cotton and wool *will*.

For individual plants, several commercial self-watering containers and less expensive reservoirs are available from commercial vendors. Individual reservoirs may be made from a variety of plastic containers, such as margarine tubs. Glass containers may also be used, but algae will build up inside clear containers; this is not harmful to the plants but is not aesthetically pleasing.

"Egg crating," sold as fluorescent light diffusers, may be purchased in 2' x 4' pieces from home-improvement stores. It can be cut to fit inside wicking trays or cut to fit across the tops of several trays. The wicks are inserted through the 1/2" squares and should be cut long enough to lie on the bottom of the tray.

These community reservoir trays may be filled with water to the top of the egg-crating (or the top of the trays if egg-crating is laid across the top of trays). The wicks draw up water as needed. Care should be taken not to let the wicks dry out or they will cease to "wick" and the plant must be either top- or bottom-watered to re-establish the capillary action in the wick.

MAT WATERING

Mat watering is a time- and space-saver. As with wicking, the plants are watered by capillary action. Pots need to have a flat bottom so the holes in the pot sit directly on the matting. Any number of materials can be used for matting: acrylic blanket, acrylic felt, light synthetic

carpet or acrylic fleece. Do not use any type of cotton or wool material. Some different types of matting are available from the commercial vendors listed in the *African Violet Magazine*. It is not necessary to use any type of wicking when mat watering; however, if the pots do not have flat bottoms that make good contact with the matting, wicks should be used.

One method for matting is to cut egg-crating to loosely fit the tray. Then cut the matting material a bit larger so it will wrap around the crating on the long sides and extend to the bottom of the tray. The tray should then be filled with enough water to keep the matting moist. Matting may also be used without egg-crating, but water will need to be added more often. Some commercial matting has a plastic layer with many tiny holes. This plastic layer has the advantage of cutting down on evaporation.

Algae may build-up in matting. This will not harm the plants but it will look unsightly and have an unpleasant odor. Simply wash the matting in a bleach solution and rinse very thoroughly. An algaecide may be put in the water as a preventative.

CAUTION: *Community trays used for wick or mat watering also serve as super-highways for soil or root dwelling pests such as soil mealybugs. Be sure your plants are pest free before introducing them to a community tray.*

TEXAS-STYLE METHOD

The Texas-Style potting and watering method was developed in Texas in the late 1970's. Texas-Style consists basically of a shallow layer of coarse, pebbly, inert material such as perlite and a shallow layer of potting mix. The plants are watered from the bottom with a dilute fertilizer solution.

A series of quarter inch holes are punched around a tub pot at the juncture of the perlite and soil mix layers. The holes may be spaced from 1" apart on 4" pots, up to 1-1/2" apart on larger pots. The depth depends on the size of the pot. The holes should be large enough so tools such as ice picks or nut picks may be inserted into them.

The holes are not to provide aeration to the root system; sufficient aeration is supplied through the exposed surface of the soil, the shallow layer of perlite, and air entering from the holes in the bottom of the pot. Texas-Style will work without the additional holes, but they do serve several purposes:

1. The depth of the perlite is indicated for potting-up purposes.

2. The depth of the perlite will be evident when adding water to the saucers.

3. A tool can be pushed through the holes to lift up the root ball and loosen it from the pot. The perlite layer is usually not saved when repotting.

DEMAND: Each plant is watered when it needs or demands it. Need is determined by the heft of the pot and the feel of the top of the soil. This method is impractical for the grower who has more than just a few plants. Each plant would have to be checked almost daily.

VISUAL REPLACEMENT: The plants are potted Texas-Style using 1-1/2" of perlite (the minimum requirement for this method of watering). A dilute fertilizer solution is added to the saucer, which should be about two inches larger than the diameter of the pot. When the solution

has been used up (no longer visible), another quarter inch of solution is added to the saucer.

SCHEDULE: Any grower with more than just a few plants should have a schedule. The pot type and the weather determine the schedule. The watering intervals can be predicted accurately within a day or two. This, combined with the margin for error provided by Texas-Style, gives an almost foolproof way to water. The interval between watering can be adjusted by a day or two to accommodate changes in the weather; however, this should not vary much since the violet room should be kept at a reasonably even temperature and humidity all year.

WATERING SCHEDULE: On the scheduled watering day, a fully rooted, mature plant, or any plant where the soil is barely moist, receives the maximum amount of water. A young plant with a just-developing root system, or any plant where the soil is still quite moist, receives just enough water to keep it going until the next scheduled watering day.

Some growers water all of their plants on the same day. Others prefer to set up a schedule for each type of container they use. Either way, it is important to post a watering schedule in the plant room. You will be amazed at how quickly four days or even six days will pass. Choosing a separate schedule for each type of pot may mean more frequent watering times; however, the length of time spent watering will be shorter. This plan may be even better with a busy grower's schedule.

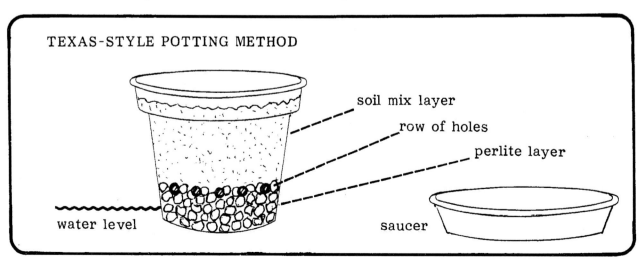

TEXAS-STYLE POTTING METHOD

soil mix layer
row of holes
perlite layer
water level
saucer

SELF-WATERING PLANTERS

The first pot on the market designed specifically for growing African violets Texas-Style was the Oyama Planter®, developed by Clem Oyama, a native of Japan and a resident of California. Rather than the usual saucer, the outer pot served as a watering saucer and also retained humidity around the inner pot. There was still ample aeration to the roots, but the interval between watering was extended. The pot appeared to be a one-piece unit.

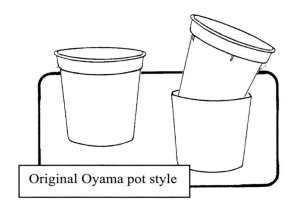

Original Oyama pot style

The original pot had an outer pot, which served as a saucer. Water was added to depths indicated by various lines molded into the outer pot. The design has since been altered so that the outer pot acts more like a reservoir than a saucer. This was accomplished by changing the lower portion of the inner pot to a pedestal-type foot, allowing for a greater volume of water in the outer pot and up to two additional days between watering.

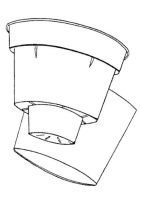

Altered design with pedestal type foot.

The pedestal foot is filled with perlite and acts like a wick, taking up the water in the reservoir as the plant needs it. The perlite layer also extends up into the top portion of the pot about 1/2" to provide additional aeration to the root system. These self-watering planters are available in a variety of sizes from 1-1/2" up to 6".

Swift Moist-Rite Planters® are square shaped self-watering planters with a large water storage reservoir allowing long intervals between watering. Small outlet holes near the inside bottom edge of the inner pot allow the plant to draw moisture as required. The automatic system is vacuum controlled to properly moisten the soil.

Optimara sells self-watering devices designed for 4" standards (MaxiWell), and 1" super miniatures (MiniWell). The Optimara Watermaid® contains an absorbent matting that draws water from the saucer into the soil.

Dandy Pots are small plastic wicking pots that sit on top of a doughnut shaped translucent reservoir. The translucent base allows growers to see when the water level is getting low and needs to be replenished. They are available in several colors.

A variety of decorative ceramic planters are sold on the Internet. These two-piece ceramic pots usually have an outer pot of glazed ceramic and an unglazed inner pot. The plant pulls moisture through the sides and bottom of the unglazed inner pot, which may or may not provide the right amount of moisture. Before purchasing this type of pot, be sure the inner pot has a drainage hole.

Pot types, layering, watering

POT TYPE	perlite layer	soil layer	free space	pot depth	water depth	watering interval
2 1/2" pot	1/2"	1 1/2"	1/4"	2 1/4"	variable	3 to 4 days
4" tub	1"	1 3/4"	3/4"	3 1/2"	1/4" to 1/2"	4 to 5 days
5" tub	1"	2 1/4"	3/4"	4"	1/4" to 1/2"	4 to 5 days
6", 7", 8", tub	1 1/4"	2 1/2"	3/4"	4 1/2"	1/4" to 1/2"	5 to 6 days
4" Oyama	1 3/4"	2"	3/4"	4 1/2" inner pot	line 1 or 2 outer pot	5 to 6 days
5" Oyama	1 1/2"	2"	3/4"	4 1/4" inner pot	line 1 or 2 outer pot	5 to 6 days
6" Oyama	1 3/4"	2 1/4"	3/4"	4 3/4" inner pot	line 1 or 2 outer pot	6 to 7 days

PERLITE LAYER: For water to draw up into the soil mix properly, the depth of the perlite should not exceed 3" in any size pot.

SOIL LAYER: The soil layer needs to be deep enough to allow potting down a 1/2" long neck and still retain enough root system so there is no shock to the plant.

FREE SPACE: The free space needs to be deep enough so the petioles are level with and rest upon the rim of the pot.

POT DEPTH: Sizes given for tub pots are approximate. Depths may vary slightly from manufacturer to manufacturer.

WATER DEPTH: The measurements given for tub pots are with the pot left in the saucer. Water refers to dilute fertilizer solution.

WATERING INTERVALS: The intervals given are for fluorescent light growing and top or bottom watering methods. It may be necessary to add one or two days to the schedule for natural light growing since growth will be somewhat slower. Be sure to change the watering schedule with the seasons. A six-day interval may be fine for winter but may have to be shortened to five days for warmer weather. Also, plants in full bloom require more water than usual. Therefore, in the weeks before a show, plants may have to be watered more frequently.

Potting Up

Every procedure practiced on show plants must be gradual and consistent. The result should be good symmetry with no breaks in the leaf size or pattern of the foliage. So, whether potting up or potting down, the goal is to pot at the right time using the right technique.

TIMING OF POTTING UP

Determining the proper time to pot up standard-sized, single-crowned plants can be based on the diameter of the foliage and the length of time the plant has grown in a pot. The general rule is to repot about every two months: two months in a 2-1/2" pot, two months in a 4" pot, and two months in a 5" pot. Unless it is a variety you have chosen to maintain in a 5" pot, it is then potted into a 6" pot and perhaps on into a 7" or 8" pot in another two months.

This kind of gradual progression allows the foliage to progress in size at an even rate. If a plant remains in one size pot for too long, the roots will crowd just enough so that the foliage shows a variation in leaf size when it is potted up to the next size.

If, at the end of the two months, the roots haven't developed sufficiently to form a root ball, it is too soon to pot the plant up. The root ball does not have to be dense, but must be formed enough to hold together when transferring the plant into the next size pot. If you are a beginner and unsure about the plant's being the right size with the right amount of root formation, the time may be extended to every three months. If it hasn't made enough progress in that length of time, you should go back and review culture procedures.

The quality of new varieties should be studied while the plants are in 4" pots. You may decide not to pot them up if the potential for good symmetry and floriferousness is not present to

some degree. Some varieties will prove to be worthy of further testing in a 5" pot.

When a grower compares a 4" pot to a 5" pot, the difference in size seems insignificant. The grower may be tempted to pot a plant from a 4" pot to a 6" pot to save repotting time. But the *volume* of a 5" pot is almost double that of a 4" pot, and the volume of a 6" pot is over three times that of a 4" pot.

For example, the cubic volumes of round standard pots are:

        3" pot = 21.2 cubic inches
        4" pot = 50.3   "   "
        5" pot = 98.2   "   "
        6" pot =169.6 "   "

When a plant in a 4" pot is potted into a 6" pot, oversized rows of leaves begin developing. Since these leaves will be noticeably larger than the outer leaves, the outer ones will soon have to be removed and no time will have been saved.

MOLD POTTING

Growers have developed a special technique for potting up so that there is little trauma to the plant's root system. It is called *mold potting*. A pot identical (or close) in size to the one in which the plant has been growing is placed inside a larger pot and new potting mix is packed around it. The smaller pot is then removed, and a hole the same size as the root ball remains. This is also a clean way to pot up. Once this potting skill is developed, there shouldn't be even a crumb of soil mix on petioles or leaves

When potting up, always loosen the root ball in a pot from the bottom. It is too risky to loosen it from the top by running a knife down between the root ball and the sides of the pot. One slip of the knife can sever a major leaf and it takes months to grow the foliage out to good symmetry again.

Try to pot just before watering day. The petioles are less turgid and, therefore, less apt to snap off.

DIRECTIONS FOR MOLD POTTING

1. Write the plant's name and the date on the selected pot, put the proper depth of perlite into it, and set the smaller pot on top of the perlite. Add moist potting mix around the inner pot and press it down firmly enough to hold in place, but not packed too tightly.

The mix should equal the density of the root ball and hold its shape when the inner pot is removed. Loosen the inner pot and set it aside.

2. Gently remove the plant from the pot. The plant will come out of the pot more easily if the potting mix is slightly dry. An unsharpened pencil or dowel can be used to gently push up through the bottom holes of the pot to lift the root ball. Lift up the root ball until the plant is loosened from the pot.

3. Remove the plant and cut off or brush away the perlite layer from the root ball. At this point, the root ball is more shallow than the hole is deep. Add enough potting mix to the hole so that the plant can be seated at the proper depth.

4. Place the root ball in the prepared hole and press it into place so that the roots make good contact with the newly added potting mix. The petioles of the lower leaves should come straight out from the main stem and rest on the rim of the pot.

    Seating the plant at the right depth in the pot is important. Proper symmetry can't be achieved if the petioles are at an upward or downward angle. The free space at the top of the pot should be about 3/4" for most varieties. This depth also allows soil to be added around a neck resulting from the removal of the first row of leaves. The exceptions are those varieties that grow in a slightly upright pattern. They have to be seated somewhat deeper in the pot so that the petioles rest on the rim of the pot at the proper angle. Free space for these varieties is then about one inch.

5. Place the plant in a saucer containing a solution of Superthrive ® (ten drops to one gallon of plain water) until the soil is completely soaked. This solution helps avoid transplant shock. At the time of the next watering, fertilize as usual.

If you misjudge and the plant is seated too high or too low in the pot, don't leave it that way. Take the plant out of the pot and redo it.

POTTING UP PLANTLETS

Plantlets may be potted up from the propagating leaf from the time their leaves are dime-sized to the time that they are half-grown plants. The best size is when plantlets are about 1-1/2" tall. Of course miniature varieties will be smaller, usually when the plantlets are about 1" across. While it is not recommended, it is possible to keep clumps for as long as two years before potting up the plantlets by using the same technique used for storing show plants (See Storing Show Plants, p. 98). Somewhere along the line, the mother leaf gets tired of mothering and gives up. The plantlets are sorry-looking specimens, but a spark of life remains. When they are finally potted up, they shape up and make rapid progress.

STEPS TO FOLLOW:
1. Pull the propagating leaf away from the clump of plantlets. If the leaf does not pull away easily, cut through the petiole, dividing it in half. Pull the plantlets apart until they are separated individually and pull away any long strings of roots.

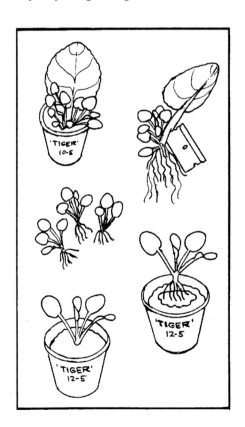

2. Write the plant's name and the date on a 2-1/2" pot, add half an inch of perlite, and fill the pot with potting mix. If wick watering, insert the wick before adding the perlite. With your finger, form a depression in the mix about 1" wide and 1-1/2" deep. Dangle the plantlet over this depression and fill in around the roots with leaf start mix. This provides a neutral medium around the delicate roots and they soon catch hold and expand into the potting mix. Firm the mix around the plantlet making sure that the crown of the plant is not covered with soil.

Place the pot in a saucer containing a solution of Superthrive (ten drops to the gallon of plain water) until the soil is well soaked. Place the pot on a community tray under lights. At the time of the next watering and for the next month or two, fertilize with 20-20-20 or similar formula. The new root system needs the stimulus of a high-nitrogen formula. When good growth has been established, follow the usual recommendations for fertilizing.

Potting Down

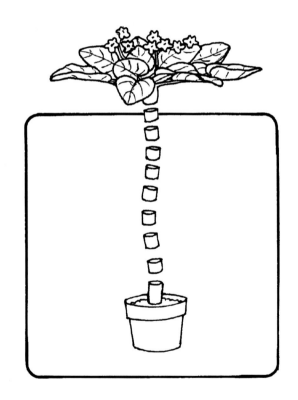

"Potting down" has two meanings among growers. Sometimes it is used to mean potting from a larger pot into a smaller one; this process (often called "recycling") becomes necessary only if a plant has been potted up too soon and the immature root system can't cope with the added volume of potting mix. The plant does poorly and has to be potted back down to a smaller-sized pot so it can be started over.

The other meaning of potting down is "getting rid of a neck." A neck will develop when natural aging and the resulting loss of leaves cause a bare stem (something like a tiny corncob) to appear below the remaining leaves. New (or *very* casual) growers will sometimes allow the neck to increase until it reaches a length of many inches! Experienced growers, who frequently remove healthy leaves to improve symmetry, know that even a short neck *must* be dealt with. Any plant with a neck that gets to be half or three-quarters of an inch long should be repotted; show plants may require being potted down three or four times a year.

RECYCLING

If properly grown, an African violet never deteriorates or wears out. Through a constant recycling process there is no limit to its life span. If a plant finds a home with a family that has an African violet grower in each generation, the plant can be passed down indefinitely from one generation to the next.

There have been reports of the same African violets being grown for fifteen to twenty-five years. Following the procedures on the following pages will guarantee indefinite life to your favorite plants.

Even though a variety can be perpetuated through leaf cuttings, a slight variation may sometimes occur and the quality of the original plant is lost. Thus, once you acquire a superb show specimen, it usually pays to keep recycling it.

POTTING DOWN A NECK

The potting-down process involves removing the plant from the pot, cutting off the bottom of the root ball equal to the length of the neck, putting the plant back into the same pot, and adding fresh potting mix around the neck. New roots quickly form around the neck and grow into the new mix. This is not the time to pot up. The plant is always placed back into a clean pot of the same size. Try to pot down just before watering day. The petioles are less turgid and, therefore, not as likely to snap off.

1. Before removing the plant from the pot, scrape (like you would a carrot) the brown scar tissue off the neck with a knife. If desired, brush a whisper of rooting powder all around the surface. Take the plant out of the pot and cut off the perlite layer.

2. From the remaining root ball, cut an amount equal to the length of the neck. The safest way is to place the plant flat on the work surface. Slide your hand under the foliage, hold the long neck between your index and middle finger, and slice evenly through the root ball. Brush away about 1/4" of the old topsoil. This eliminates the layer of mix where most of the fertilizer salts accumulate.

When plants have had a neck potted down many times, the main stem eventually extends the full depth of the root ball. This stem must be cut through each time the plant is potted down.

3. Put new perlite in the bottom of the pot and place the plant back in the pot. It should be seated in the pot so that the petioles of the lower leaves come straight out from the main stem and rest on the rim of the pot. With the leaf lifter in place, fill in around the neck with fresh soil up to the lowest row of petioles. Gently press the potting mix down, being careful to not pack too firmly.

If the plant has a crooked neck, bury the neck so it is straight up and down. The plant will correct itself and begin growing straight within a few weeks and it won't be lop-sided.

LEAF LIFTER

Using a leaf lifter will save much brushing and cleaning of soil particles from petioles and under leaves. The lifter also distributes the pressure along the petioles when lifting the foliage so that the chance of snapping off a petiole at the main stem is lessened. Brush off soil particles from pot rim and side before removing the leaf lifter from under the foliage.

Make a leaf lifter from a piece of 5" x 8" sturdy cardboard and shape it into a slight curve. Grasp the edge of the lifter between three fingers and the thumb and slip it under the foliage about 1-1/2" from the neck. Place your little finger under the lifter and hook it over the edge of the pot to keep the pot in place as you gently lift the foliage. Spoon the potting mix into the potting mix into the pot under the lifter. As you work, be sure the plant remains centered in the pot.

SHOCK REVIVAL METHOD

Once you become adept at cultural methods, having a plant or leaf go into shock happens so rarely that you will be almost as shocked as the plant. Occasionally you will be aware of the risk and will keep an eye out for it, such as when you pot down the neck of a plant when it has become so long that only a thin slice of root ball remains. But other times, you may put down a half dozen leaves and a few hours later one of them takes a nosedive and hangs over the edge of the pot like a limp tongue. Why this leaf? Or why this time?

Use the miracle of humidity to revive plants or leaves that have gone into shock; a giant show plant can be revived when the leaves are discovered hanging limply over the support ring a few hours after potting down a neck. Keep a supply of plastic bags of various sizes on hand. Bag the leaf or plant, pot and all, and close the top of the bag with a wire twist. Within a few days, the leaf or foliage should be crisp again. Wait a week or ten days and then remove the bag completely. For large plants, plastic dry-cleaner bags work well. They are lightweight, large enough for good coverage and can be tucked under foliage so that high humidity is maintained. Another source of plastic sheeting is the lightest-weight painter's drop cloths.

If the foliage hasn't perked up in two or three days, chances are that the plant will not recover. The variety can be rescued by restarting the center crown.

RESTARTING A CROWN

There will be times when foliage has been damaged to such an extent that the plant must be stripped down to the center crown and started over. It takes so long to grow out the damaged leaves that the plant shouldn't be taking up valuable space during the process.

There are two reasons why it is advantageous to restart a plant from a crown rather than from a leaf cutting. First, the process is much faster. Plants grow back to exhibition size from a crown in about four or five months, whereas, it takes from six to eight months from a leaf cutting. Second, there is less risk of losing the characteristics of the variety.

Occasionally a sport occurs from a crown, but is more likely to happen when propagating from a leaf cutting. The sported characteristics may be slight, such as the loss of a colored or frilled edge. Other times the resulting plantlets may be completely different from the original plant.

The following are accidental or cultural problems that could necessitate restarting a plant from a crown:

1. There has been major damage to the leaves of an inner row. One damaged leaf can be tolerated unless it is a particularly ugly mar or tear.

2. An off-sized upper row of leaves occurs due to a lapse in cultural procedures.

3. A neck has become so long that the plant cannot be potted down safely.

4. The center leaves are burned from over fertilizing. This is an occasional problem with sensitive varieties even though they are on the same fertilizing program as the rest of the collection.

THE PROCEDURE: Once the decision has been made to restart the crown, there is no point in trying to save all the foliage. The foliage that is retained will shrink while the stub of the crown is putting out new roots and will eventually have to be removed. This is a different procedure from that of putting down a three-leafed crown when storing a plant for an indefinite time (See Storing Show Plants, p. 98). In this case, rapid results are desired so that the plant will be back to maturity as soon as possible. Thus, more leaves are retained in order to speed up the physiological processes that form the new roots and growth of foliage.

1. Strip away all foliage except five or six center leaves. Cut the main stem to 1-1/2" to 2" and scrape the neck. Brush a sprinkling of rooting powder around the stub (optional).

2. Prepare a 3" pot. Fill with potting mix. Using your finger, make a well approximately 1-1/2" wide by 2" deep in the center of the mix. Hold the stub in the well and fill in around it with leaf start or potting mix. Bottom water until mix is just damp.

3. Place the pot in a plastic bag, expand the bag by blowing into it, twist the top shut, and secure tightly with a wire twist. Leave the bag closed for two weeks. Open and loosen the top of the bag for another two weeks, then remove it. When the plant is large enough, pot it into a 4" pot. Remove the off-sized outer row of leaves as soon as growth is well established.

SALVAGING A DAMAGED-CROWN

Excess fertilizer may cause the center leaves in the crown to become damaged and appear burned. The center leaves will be small and fail to grow properly. The plant can be saved if the damage is not so severe that the crown is lost.

Leach the soil with plain water and allow the damaged leaves to grow out until they are in the position of the second row from the center and a new crown has formed. The damaged row of leaves can then be removed and the new crown soon fills the gap. This strategy is usually more successful with wavy or ruffled-leaf varieties. The size difference in the rows of leaves on a variety with plain foliage may remain noticeable.

PLANT & LEAF RESUSCITATION

Survival is one of the strongest traits that is biologically programmed into plants – even to so-called delicate plants like African violets. When a plant looks hopelessly dead or a leaf cutting hopelessly wilted, there is a good chance that a spark of life still exists.

Most growers have had an experience involving a plant that was neglected, perhaps in a terrarium that was shoved under a work table after a show only to be discovered several months later bone dry; the plant would be a limp, sad specimen and the leaves leathery but not crackling dry. If the room had good humidity and wasn't too hot, there is a chance the plant could be resuscitated by stripping it down to a stub, putting it in moist starter mix in a 2-1/2" pot, bagging it, and placing it under lights. The top of the bag should be loosened three or four weeks later and left open for another three or four weeks. When the crown shows fresh, new growth, pot it into a 4" pot. In spite of this ordeal, plants have been known to live to go to another show.

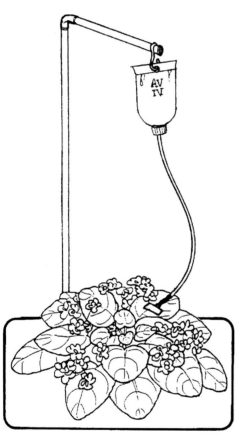

Another scenario of neglect could involve a leaf cutting of a choice variety that was received as a last minute gift or purchased at a show and stuck in a box or luggage; a week or so later the leaf was discovered laying loose on tissue paper with no wrapping or bag, about as limp as a leaf could get. Limp leaves can be resuscitated by cutting the end on a diagonal in order to expose as much cut surface as possible and completely submerging the leaf in a saucer of warm water. The leaf should be left until it becomes turgid

and crisp enough to work with; this may take several days. The leaf may then be potted according to the usual method; take the additional precaution of putting the potted leaf in a plastic bag. Loosen the top of the bag after about ten days and remove it entirely in another ten days. It may take a long time for a plantlet to pop up.

Whether dealing with the near-death of a favorite plant or a hard-to-get variety, don't give up until you have given resuscitation methods a chance.

MENDING PETIOLES & LEAVES

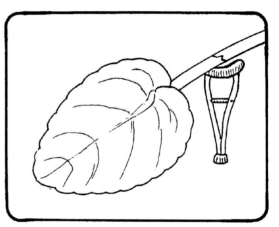

Any time plants are potted or groomed, there is always the risk that a petiole or leaf may be broken. A petiole that is partially broken can sometimes be saved if there is a portion of tissue or "skin" still connecting the two sections. Carefully prop the leaf so that the broken tissue is pressed firmly together in its original position.

Even if the break heals, the leaf may atrophy and be off-sized; but this procedure may save the symmetry of a plant until the leaf can be grown out and removed. Flag the plant and avoid handling it for a week or so.

A cracked leaf may also heal if the edges are pressed together and held in position for a week or so. Place a piece of tape underneath the leaf and carefully position the cracked edges together. Remove the tape before exhibiting the plant in a judged show.

Several methods of propagation can be used to reproduce African violets—seeds, leaf cuttings, blossom stems, and suckers. Some hobbyists like to grow a few of the species, but the plants most of us grow are exclusively hybrids. The species reproduce true from seed, but hybrids can only be reproduced vegetatively.

The cross breeding of two varieties is a fascinating field, but it is not one to explore for those with limited space. As many as 150 seeds may germinate from one seedpod. Each plantlet must be grown to flowering size in order to determine its potential. Otherwise, the great new blossom color of the decade may be missed! And, out of those 150 plants, perhaps only one or two will be worth saving. It takes a lot of discipline to throw away 148 blooming plants.

Most hobbyist growers are interested in reproducing only specific hybrid varieties that will make good show plants. Thus, the two methods of propagation for this purpose are leaf cuttings and suckers. Commercial growers propagate only chimeras from suckers, but suckers provide a rapid means for amateur growers to exchange new varieties with friends.

LEAF CUTTINGS

Many growers use their regular soilless potting mix for starting leaves; however, others use a leaf start mix composed of one part perlite and one part vermiculite. Mix, dampen, and store this mix in a plastic bag or pail. It keeps indefinitely.

Mature leaves of an intermediate size produce the best plantlets. Fresh, immature leaves can also be used for propagating, but avoid using old leaves whenever possible. Using a rooting hormone is a personal preference. Many growers feel that plantlets seem to come up sooner without use of a rooting powder on leaf cuttings. Rooting hormone seems to promote a pot full of roots and plantlets take a long time to appear.

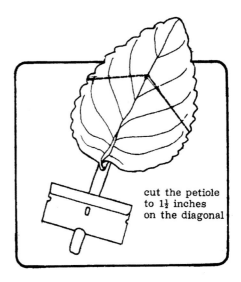

cut the petiole to 1½ inches on the diagonal

1. Cut the end of the petiole diagonally with a very sharp razor blade. Leave about 1" to 1-1/2" of petiole. Plantlets develop from the cut end of the petiole and if the petiole is too long, they have too great a distance to grow in order to reach the light. If the leaf is one-of-a-kind and the petiole is accidentally broken off, the base of the leaf can be cut in a "V" shape to create a new "petiole."

2. Use 1-1/2" pots or 3 oz. plastic drinking cups with holes punched in the bottom. Write the plant's name and the date on the pot. Fill the pot with damp mix. Pack it down firmly and water with fertilizer solution.

3. Make a hole in the mix with a pencil or similar tool. Place the petiole in the hole so that the mix is almost up to the bottom of the leaf; firm the mix around the petiole. Place the pots under lights in a community tray or individual saucers. Water from the bottom using regular fertilizer solution.

Sometimes leaves are too large to pot properly or will continue to grow after potting. In this case, cut a segment off the top of the leaf. This stops growth, and energy will go to producing plantlets.

Unless you are growing plants for sale, you will not need the five to fifteen plantlets produced by each leaf cutting. When the plantlets start appearing, pick off all but a few of the biggest ones. This gives you one or two extras to share with friends, but you won't be taking up space growing a lot of duplicates. However, if you are growing plants to sell, you will want to produce as many plantlets as possible from each leaf. There may be different cutting and potting techniques that increase production. Consult with experienced growers.

PROPAGATING TRAILERS

Trailers may be propagated by leaf cuttings but a crown cutting is the fastest method of producing a new plant. The procedure for starting a cutting is the same as for starting suckers except a stem can be created by removing some of the lower leaves of the cutting.

PROPAGATING SUCKERS

While excessive suckering can be the result of poor culture, damage, or disease, some suckering is to be expected when plants are constantly pushed to their peak of growth and flowering. Take advantage of an occasional sucker by allowing it to become large enough to propagate. The sucker should have four leaves and measure about 1-1/2" (either tall or across). Don't allow suckers to become so large that they spoil the symmetry of the parent plant.

There are advantages to propagating from suckers. You will have a plant much sooner than by putting down a leaf and plants propagated this way are almost certain to come true to the parent plant. In the case of chimeras, it is the only way for the hobbyist to get a true reproduction.

1. Use a Sucker Plucker (or similar tool) to remove suckers intact from the plant. Suckers that form at the base of the main stem at the soil line usually are rooted in the soil; in this case, slip the triangular end of the tool between the sucker and the main stem. Cut straight down until the sucker separates. Then loosen the roots from the soil. If you leave a few roots attached, growth will be much more rapid.

2. Removing a sucker intact that has formed in the axil of a petiole requires some delicate surgery. One slip and a major leaf can be severed. Again using the triangular end, make partial cuts all around the base of the sucker, cut carefully between the sucker and petiole and between the sucker and main stem until it is loose. If the sucker is small enough, it may pop out of the axil by pushing at the base of it with a pencil. To encourage root formation, you may wish to brush rooting powder on the cut end of the sucker.

3. Write the plant name and the date on the pot and fill it with moist leaf start or potting mix. Press the mix down firmly and water with fertilizer solution. Make a shallow trough in the top of the mix and lay the sucker in this indentation. Push the sucker down gently so it makes good contact with the mix but not so deeply that the center is buried.

4. Place the pot in a plastic bag, expand the bag slightly by blowing into it, twist the top shut, and secure with a wire twist. Leave the bag closed for two or three weeks. Open and loosen the top of the bag for another two weeks, then remove the bag. Be sure to water the plant during the two-week open-bag period. When the plant is large enough, pot it into a 4" pot.

PROPAGATING CHIMERAS

These striped-blossomed sports do not reproduce true from leaf cuttings. The usual method is to reproduce a chimera from a sucker, but suckers don't always form at the base of the plant when you would like. With a little expertise and luck, most varieties can be propagated from a blossom stem cutting. However, this method is slow and only two plants (suckers) will produce from each stem cutting.

Occasionally chimeras fail to reproduce true even when propagated from suckers or blossom stem cuttings.

BLOSSOM STEM CUTTINGS:
1. Cut the peduncle of a fresh bloom stalk about 1" below the two leafy "ears" that are beneath the cluster of pedicels. The larger the leaf ears, the greater the chance of success. Trim the pedicels close to the two leaves and dip the peduncle in rooting powder.

2. Put the prepared blossom stem in a pot of moistened leaf start mix up to the leaf ears. Place the pot in a plastic bag and leave the bag closed until new plants form in the axils on either side of the stem.

As soon as the new plants are fully formed and about 1-1/2" tall, cut them away from the propagating stem and put them down to root following the directions for rooting suckers.

With the rapid advances being made in tissue culture, chimeras may soon come down in price. In the meantime, take good care of these costly varieties. Some of them are stable, but on others, the blossoms may revert to a plain color if the soil is allowed to dry out too often.

PRODUCING MULTIPLE SUCKERS: Since chimeras sell for many times the price of regular varieties, you may want to reproduce as many plants as possible. Pinching out the crown of a single-crowned variety can produce multiple suckers. (Keep one or two rows of leaves in order to ensure the survival of the plant.) Within a few weeks as many as four or five suckers will form. Remove them when they are big enough to pot up. Scrape away any scar tissue that has formed in the crown and a new crop of suckers will grow.

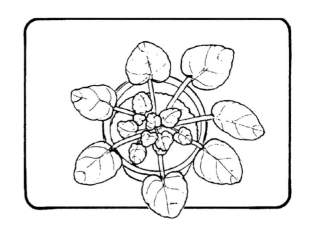

HOW TO PLANT A LEAF

1. Cut the stem diagonally 1/2" to 1-1/2" from the bottom of the leaf (front side) with a sharp knife or razor blade.

2. Place entire leaf in tepid water for 2 hours before potting.

3. Label a small 2" or 2-1/2" pot with plant name and date.

4. Fill pot with damp potting mix or leaf start mix. Pack down firmly and water with dilute fertilizer solution.

5. Poke a 1/4" hole in moistened mix.

6. Insert stem so that the mix is almost up to the bottom of the leaf and firm the mix around the stem.

7. Place potted leaf in a small plastic bag or clear plastic box with lid; keep humidity high.

8. Place under lights or in a window, but do not put in direct sunlight; they will cook!

9. Water as needed with fertilizer solution. Do not allow the mix to dry out.

10. Plantlets will start to appear in about 6 weeks; some varieties take longer.

11. If the "mother" leaf continues to grow, cut the top off the leaf so the energy goes to the plantlets.

12. If several small plantlets emerge (some leaves will produce 5 to 15 plantlets) remove the weaker ones and leave two or three on the mother leaf until they have four nickel size leaves. When plantlets are about 1-1/2" tall, pot into 2-1/2" pots.

Grooming For Symmetry

"Symmetry" means more than just the outer leaf-tips touching an imaginary circle. It means the way the leaves and rows of leaves overlap each other, the straightness of the petioles, the evenness of the spacing of foliage around the stem, and the way each layer of leaves is, from crown to outer edge, progressively larger than the layer that follows.

A grower cannot create symmetry where none exists; the degree of symmetry a plant can achieve is a basic characteristic of each variety. Symmetry can, however, be improved by the application of various techniques. Grooming is one of them.

Because of its complexity, grooming is usually one of the last skills that new growers attempt to learn. A beginner is usually reluctant to remove any leaf for fear it will be wrong; once a leaf is removed, it can never be re-attached, right? And the beginner is so proud of having grown a plant to a substantial size that it almost seems a sacrilege to start removing what appear to be perfectly good leaves. Nevertheless, this skill must be acquired and the only way is through practice.

Just as the word *practice* implies, mistakes will be made while you are learning. Relax! A mistake can be grown out in a few months, and the plant will be as good as new. At first the decision to remove even one leaf will be agonizingly slow, but you soon will be able to strip away an entire row of unwanted leaves in a matter of minutes.

THE PATTERN OF THREE

As new leaves emerge from the crown, they form a distinct pattern of three. They do not emerge simultaneously, they are not equal in size, and they do not form an equilateral triangle (all sides equal). Rather, they form a scalene triangle (three unequal sides). You need to train your eye to see this particular triangular pattern.

Each row of leaves consists of several groups of this series of three.

The pattern of three is fairly easy to recognize on young plants but becomes more difficult to discern as the plant matures. When one immature leaf is spotted, always look for the other two. Perhaps one or both were removed during previous grooming, but it pays to look.

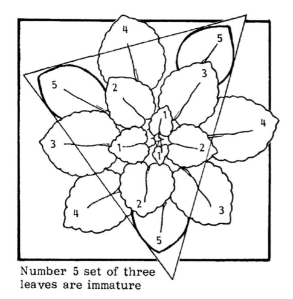

Number 5 set of three leaves are immature

69

RECOGNIZING IMMATURE LEAVES

Immature leaves (which are not to be confused with off-sized leaves) are always found in the outermost row of leaves. As plantlets emerge from the base of the mother leaf, the first leaves to form are immature (baby) leaves. Eventually sturdy, true leaves begin to form and the immature ones progress to the outer row.

As each succeeding row of leaves progresses outward there will be a set of three leaves that, while mature at one time, stop developing at the same rate as the other leaves in the same row. This lack of development becomes apparent as these leaves reach the outermost row. This is a natural occurrence; as new leaves form, older ones fade and die. Thus, each leaf is pro-grammed to (eventually) self-destruct. Three-by-three they reach a stage where development slows and, if not removed by the grower, will naturally weaken and die.

CLUES TO LOOK FOR:

Leaf size: The leaves are smaller than the others in the same row.

Petiole size: Petioles are smaller, weaker, and paler in color.

Leaf texture: Leaves are not as deeply quilted, as curly, or as wavy, according to the variety.

Suckers: Suckers often form at the base of the petiole of an immature leaf.

REMOVING IMMATURE LEAVES

PLANTLET (Figure A): After plantlets have been potted up, leave immature leaves (baby leaves) on for about thirty days; they help pro-vide nourishment to the forming root system. These spindly light-colored leaves are easy to recognize.

YOUNG PLANT (Figure B): After plantlets show signs of growth and the foliage has begun to fill in, start removing immature leaves. They have served their purpose and the energy of the plant should go toward developing the more permanent leaves. Also, they often keep the maturing leaves from lying in proper position.

MATURE PLANT (Figure C): When all baby leaves (as shown in Figures A and B) are re-moved, that would seem to be the end of it, but some leaves do not continue to develop at the same rate as the others. At this stage they are much harder to spot. The following techniques will help avoid mistakes.

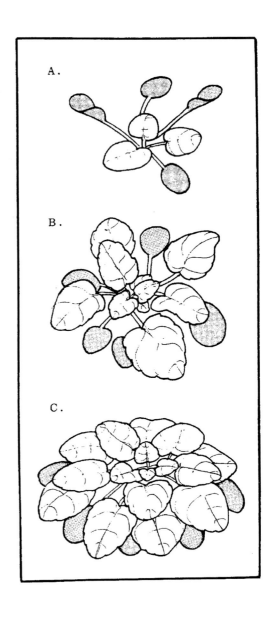

THE COVERUP TEST: Place the plant on the floor so that the pattern of the symmetry may be easily seen. When a possible pattern of three underdeveloped leaves is spotted, cover these leaves with facial tissue and observe the symmetry of the uncovered leaves. If you are still unsure, move the pieces of tissue to cover different leaves until the proper pattern becomes clear.

THE PETIOLE POSITION TEST: Make a final check to determine if the choice of leaves to be removed is correct. Visually trace the petioles back to the main stem. If they are at the lowest position on the main stem and fairly evenly spaced around the stem, the choice is probably the correct one. If any of the petioles are positioned slightly above the other, particularly in the second row up, go back and try the tissue placement test again.

REMOVING THE LEAF: Because of the angle of the petiole to the main stem and the amount of foliage, it is risky to try and cut off the petiole. The safest way to remove a leaf is to run your fingers down the full length of the petiole and snap it off at the base with your index finger.

Even after all undesirable leaves have been removed from the outermost row, instant symmetry is not always achieved; it will depend on the variety and the number of leaves that were removed. There may be an immediate improvement in symmetry on some varieties and others may take a few weeks for the circular pattern to fill in.

Properly groomed show plants rarely have more than three rows of leaves (not including the three small center leaves). The only difference between a 15" show plant and a 21" show plant is the length of the petioles and the size of the leaves.

TRIANGULAR LEAF PATTERN

Keep in mind that the triangular leaf pattern of some varieties is very pronounced and a circular pattern never forms. It doesn't matter how many leaves are removed, you simply end up with a smaller triangle. Sometimes varieties with this leaf pattern can still win a blue ribbon if the three leaves that form the outer triangle are left on until a day or so before the show. If they are removed too soon, the next set of three leaves start an accelerated rate of growth and the triangular pattern is once again prominent.

OFF-SIZED ROW OF LEAVES

Nothing detracts from the beauty of African violets more than a petticoat of off-sized, ragged, immature leaves. Plants should never go to a show in this disheveled state. Torn or spotted leaves are obvious and there are lots of clues that give away immature or underdeveloped leaves. But unless the size difference is significant, an entire row of off-sized leaves is hard for the beginner to recognize.

An off-sized row can be any row where the leaves are smaller than those of the next row above. The leaves have been stunted through one or more of the following lapses in culture (commonly referred to as a "culture break").

Not potting up at the proper time: Growth is slowed when roots reach a certain stage of density. When the plant is belatedly potted up, growth eventually accelerates. As the new leaves grow in, they form rows of larger leaves.

Not potting down a *neck soon enough:* The foliage experiences a setback. When the roots expand into the new soil, the new leaves become larger than existing ones.

Not watering plants at *the proper time:* Even though the plants survive, fine feeder roots are damaged when a plant is allowed to become too dry. Off-sized foliage is the result.

Not controlling environmental factors or *practicing consistent cultural method:* Extreme or rapid changes in light hours, weather conditions, fertilizing, soil mix formulas, etc. will result in off-sized foliage.

If the row of off-sized leaves is the outermost row, remove it and fill in around the resulting neck or, if necessary, pot the neck down. If it is on an inner row, the row must be grown out until it can be removed. If there is not time to grow it out and the plant is entered in a show, points will probably be deducted under condition. The grower must decide if the row is so noticeable that the plant would not win a blue ribbon.

WAYWARD LEAVES

Moving leaves (even if done gradually) and staking them into position in order to create better symmetry does not work. It causes a new set of problems and, in the long run, the contrary leaves must be removed.

If a wayward leaf is moved too far out of the path it has taken, there is considerable stress at the juncture of the petiole and the main stem. This causes a leaf to weaken and fail to develop further; it may even expire.

Almost without exception, a wayward or curved-petiole leaf will prove to be an immature leaf. Remove it, and within a few weeks the other leaves will usually fall into place and fill the gap. Rearranging the foliage by hand to fill in the gap sometimes results in instantly improved symmetry.

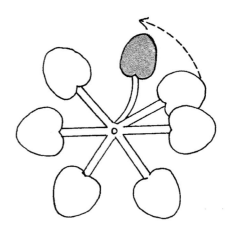

MARRED LEAVES

Marred leaves are those with any kind of unsightly damage, whether caused through a mishap or a physiological problem. Removing marred leaves may or may not improve symmetry. There are certain rules of symmetry that must be observed before leaves are removed:

INNER ROW: If a marred leaf is in an inner row, it is usually best to allow it to progress to the outer row before removing it. If only one leaf in an inner row is removed, the foliage often collapses on that side of the plant and symmetry is spoiled.

OUTERMOST ROW: The entire outermost row of leaves should be removed if there are too many marred leaves. If there are only one or two marred leaves, mentally compute (a) the number of points that may be deducted for the marred leaves and (b) how many points may be deducted for the resulting loss of symmetry if they are removed. The best strategy may be to choose leaving on the marred leaves (See AVSA Scale of Points, p. 80).

LOPSIDED FOLIAGE

Some varieties of African violets have a denser pattern of leaves on one side of the plant. It may necessitate leaving a few underdeveloped leaves on the sparse side in order to balance out the foliage. A few points may be deducted for these leaves, but more points would be deducted for lack of symmetry if they were removed.

Some plants grow lopsided because the plant was not properly centered when it was re-potted. A plant uses its roots to discover which way the leaves can grow. If the roots are up against the pot on one side, the leaves will grow in that direction and will become larger. Usually, once the plant is centered it will be fine.

REPOSITIONING FOLIAGE

CENTER LEAVES: Symmetry ultimately depends on the quality and perfection of the newly forming leaves. Show plants are partially disbudded so that new leaves are not stunted or distorted from a heavy mass of bloom. But the demands of fluorescent lights and the forcing techniques used to grow show plants sometimes causes tight centers. If the centers are not watched closely, the leaves may fold back or twist sideways. They need to be assisted in clearing the next row of leaves or be gently turned to point them back in the right direction. This has to be done at the right time. If the leaves are too small, they will snap off when lifted. If left too long, they may tear or be difficult to pull from under the preceding row.

MATURE FOLIAGE: Arrange the foliage so

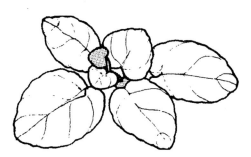

that the leaves of each row are in the proper overlapping position. Gently move leaves into position to fill in symmetry; the weight of other foliage sometimes holds them in position.

In grooming for symmetry the goal is to have a perfect circle of matching leaves on the outside row with proportionately smaller leaves comprising each of the preceding rows and forming a perfect overlapping pattern. This is part of the excitement of growing show plants– the challenge of your mind over their matter!

Training For Symmetry

Few varieties have petioles turgid enough so that the petioles maintain straight growth without using leaf support rings. Even the sturdiest varieties benefit from leaf-supports, plus the foliage is displayed at its most attractive pattern throughout the year. A leaf support should be used from the time the plant is potted into a 4" pot.

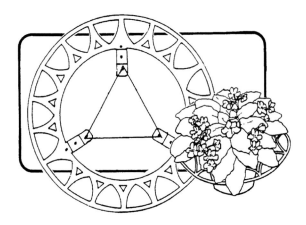

Support rings not only train petioles to grow straight but also enable the grower to arrange the placement of foliage for improved distribution around the main stem. A part of your regular grooming schedule should be the arranging of foliage, by hand, into proper position.

Petiole strength is a basic characteristic of a variety. Leaf-support rings cannot strengthen innately weak petioles. Neither will providing support weaken petioles. Petioles are not like muscles that atrophy from disuse.

Petioles normally can be expected to drop slightly when the ring is removed. If the leaves flop to the table, the variety does not have sturdy petioles to begin with (assuming the plant has been properly grown). When testing the potential of new varieties, always remove the leaf supports occasionally to see how the petioles hold up. It may prevent a rude shock at show time and you may decide to eliminate a variety before it takes up space all year.

LEAF-SUPPORT RINGS: These rings are made of heavy-duty plastic, which is a soft green that blends unobtrusively with the foliage. They attach to the pot with rubber bands and fit up to 7" pots. Use the 9" ring for foliage 8" to 14" in diameter and the 13" ring for foliage 14" to 18" in diameter.

For show plants 18" and over, you can use plastic picnic plates to make extenders. If you use cardboard, cover it with contact paper; most cardboard is porous and will draw moisture from the leaf edges, turning them brown. You can make your own leaf supports from these plastic plates. Cut one in half, then cut half circles smaller than the pot rim. Slip each half under the leaves using the pot rim to support the inner edge of the plate.

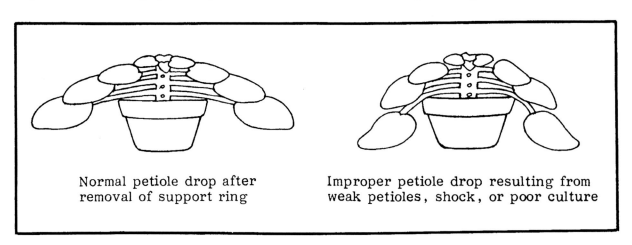

Normal petiole drop after removal of support ring

Improper petiole drop resulting from weak petioles, shock, or poor culture

Disbudding

The difference between an avid show grower and a fanatical show grower lies almost exclusively with the practice of disbudding. An avid grower can't bear *not* to see blossoms throughout the year; a fanatical grower is content to see nothing but foliage all year except when a show is near.

Colorful blossoms are what set African violets apart from ordinary houseplants. How depressing it would be to not see a blossom except for the relatively brief period when plants are brought into bloom for a show! And yet, if the plants are allowed to remain in full bloom all year, the foliage does not develop to the perfection required to win top awards. Partial disbudding is the answer. This process permits the show grower to have both blossoms and perfect foliage.

PARTIAL DISBUDDING

Using a pointed instrument, remove every second or third forming bud. Allow only one or two buds to grow to blossoming stage at one time. There will always be blossoms to admire, but most of the energy produced by the plant is directed toward the growth of foliage, and the newly forming leaves of the crown won't become distorted or stunted from heavy blooming.

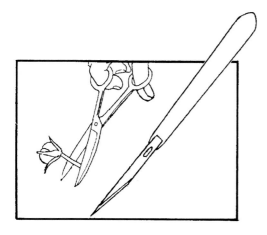

Completely snub out those buds selected for removal. If the peduncle is long enough, a fast upward jerk usually snaps it off clean at the base; this saves the tedious task of removing peduncle stubs from what will be the lowest axils on the main stem at show time. Any additional buds that may form in the axils produce only weak, undersized bloom stalks, and blossoms probably will not reach the top of the foliage. Vigorous, full-sized bloom stalks are produced only in the uppermost row of leaves.

Only one bud forms in the axils of most varieties; two buds may form in the same axil of other varieties.

COMPLETE DISBUDDING

To encourage maximum floriferousness, start completely disbudding ten weeks before show (See Pre-Show Schedule, p. 87). At this point, a scant 1/8" stub of the peduncle is left on. Use small sharp scissors, a surgical knife, or something similar; carefully avoid damaging any additional buds that may form in the same axil.

General Grooming

The grooming of show plants must be a continuous process. It is too late to start grooming plants just before show time. The foliage will have strangled on the accumulation of dust, unchecked suckers will have distorted symmetry, and one or more rows of immature or marred leaves will have accumulated. Keep up with grooming by observing the following general schedule.

Once a week (perhaps on watering day): Check for suckers. Remove excess bloom stalks, spent blossoms, and spent bloom stalks. Remove undesirable leaves and help new center leaves to lie flat. Using a natural sponge or tissue, pat up any spilled fertilizer solution from the foliage as you water. Large droplets of solution may spot sensitive foliage.

Once a month: Damp-wipe foliage.

Every two or three months: Wash foliage.

BRUSHING FOLIAGE: Because the leaves of African violets are hairy and the violet room's atmosphere is humid, *it is impossible to brush away dust without damaging the texture of the leaves.* Foliage should be brushed only to flick away soil particles (when potting), lint, animal hair, etc. Use a soft-bristled brush.

DAMP-WIPING FOLIAGE: Dust is not easily seen on African violet foliage because of the matte finish created by the hairs of the leaves. However, to remind yourself of how dust accumulates, check a table top that hasn't been dusted for a few days! It is necessary to damp-wipe foliage only about once a month. Even though some dust will have accumulated, adequate respiration is taking place from undersides of the leaves.

WASHING FOLIAGE: Wash foliage when the temperature is at least 70°F and early enough in the day so that foliage dries before the lights turn off. Take the plants to a kitchen or utility sink and run the tap until a gentle stream of tepid water flows. Hooking your thumb over the rim, grip the pot firmly with one hand. Tilt the plant so that the water doesn't run into the pot. It is not enough to just run the water over the foliage. Place the fingers of your free hand under each leaf to support it, and use your thumb to wash away embedded grime. It is NOT advisable to wash the center leaves.

Pat up excess water with a soft natural sponge (or paper towel) and place the plant back under the lights. Fluorescent light will not burn wet foliage but if large drops of water are left on the foliage, the mineral content of the water may leave permanent spots. Sometimes water spots can be removed by damp-wiping foliage with a vinegar solution (a few drops to one cup of water). Protect plants from drafts until the foliage is dry.

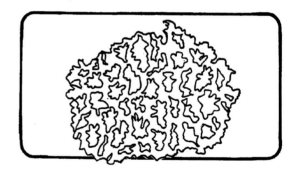

NATURAL SPONGE: A natural sea sponge is useful for damp-wiping or washing foliage or sopping up excess water; no other material does these things so well. A sponge about the size of a small orange will turn as soft as butter when wet and it fits into the curves of leaves without causing them to break or crack. Facial tissue leaves lint on the leaves. Some synthetic sponges are too stiff, and others do not absorb water readily.

Mediterranean silk wool sponges are expensive but well worth the price. Try the cosmetic sections of better department stores.

If there are quite a few plants to be washed, fill the sink with warm water and set the pot on its side on the drain board with the foliage hanging over the sink. Place one hand under the foliage. Turning the pot as you go, wash the foliage with generous amounts of water. This is the best way to wash the foliage of trailers.

REMOVING SUCKERS: Remove suckers before they become large enough to distort the symmetry of the foliage. Be especially diligent about checking for suckers before a judged show. *Judges will eliminate from consideration any single-crowned specimen that has a sucker.*

REMOVING LEAVES: The weekly watering period is not the time to study the plants' symmetry nor to take extensive corrective measures. But do remove leaves that are obviously limp, immature, or both.

REMOVING SPENT BLOSSOMS & BLOOM STALKS: Removing faded blossoms and peduncles is part of weekly grooming. Checking for (and possibly removing) excess bloom stalks should also be done weekly. Check again during final grooming, though. Removing peduncle and pedicel stubs is part of final grooming before a show.

A Check List "What the Judges Look For In A Show Plant" (p. 86) contains a list of questions every grower of show plants should answer, several times, in the weeks and days before show. Many of the questions point to correctible conditions that if remedied several weeks before show can make the difference between Best in Show and a blue or red ribbon. All of the items on the checklist are discussed in the following sections and more information may be found in the AVSA *Handbook for Growers, Exhibitors, and Judges.*

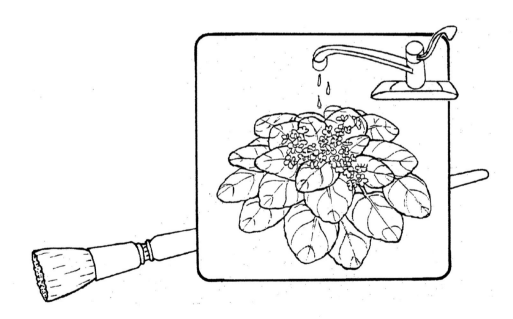

Show Plant Hints

1. Remember: Not all plants can be made into show plants. Not all plants will grow well for you. Keep only those plants which grow well in your environment.

2. Selection: For initial selection, choose previous show winners or buy new plants from a hybridizer of previous show winners. Try varieties from reliable growers.

3. Pot a new plant into your own potting mix as soon as possible. This will help to determine which new plants will grow best in your conditions.

4. When propagating from a leaf, select the strongest baby plantlets to pot up.

5. Grooming begins with baby plants. Remember the Rule of Three.

6. Pot up systematically on a schedule.

7. If a plant dries out completely (oops!), repot and restore proper moisture.

8. When potting, do not pot too shallow or too deep.

9. Have a planned schedule for potting, grooming, fertilizing, and disbudding.

10. Disbud.

11. No matter how many plants you have, potential show plants get the most attention. "Old favorites, sale plants, etc." can wait or get less attention.

12. The schedule for standards is not the same as for miniatures and semiminiatures.

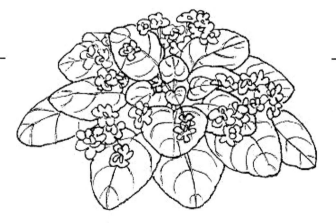

SINGLE-CROWNED STANDARDS

Standard refers to the size of a mature single-crowned plant; they may be *small standards* 8" to 10" in diameter to *large-standards,* which can be as large as 20" to 24" in diameter. The genetics of the variety as well as growing conditions dictate the ultimate size of a standard plant.

From the time the show grower starts to select show plants, when a young plant first blooms to the final selection of entries, there are a number of things to keep in mind.

SYMMETRY of the plant is one of the most important characteristics of a good show plant, whether a single-crowned standard, a miniature or semiminiature. Some varieties have naturally good symmetry; the skill of the grower is necessary to create symmetry in others. Remember the *rule of three* (See Grooming, p. 69) and start to work with potential show plants from the time they are very young plants.

QUANTITY OF BLOOM is another variable that is partly the variety and partly the growing conditions. Some plants naturally have a large number of blossoms without any special care; others require changing the fertilizer and light hours on a specific schedule. When being judged, points are deducted if the plant lacks the quantity of bloom expected on a mature specimen of the variety or if it lacks the proper number of blossoms in proportion to its foliage. It is not only the number of blossoms, but also the condition of the blossoms that is considered. Only fresh, open blossoms are counted; buds count only when seedlings and sports are judged.

Points are deducted if the blossoms are not the size expected for the variety or if the variety is not blooming true to classification. The show grower should compare the description of each show plant with the hybridizers description in the *African Violet Master List of Species and Cultivars* or *First Class.*

In judging, points are deducted if the variety is not blooming true to blossom-color description. Allowances are made for various cultural conditions and naturally occurring variations but if the blossom color is completely different from the hybridizer's description, ten points are deducted.

CONDITION (cultural perfection) of the plant is a result of growing and grooming that is under the control of the grower. Points or fractions of points are deducted for each of the following faults: spent blossoms; petiole, peduncle, and pedicel stubs; dust or other particles on foliage; yellow, bleached, immature, off-sized, or marred leaves; over- or under-potting; blossoms not evenly distributed around the crown (or around the plant, in the case of trailers); lack of proper variegation according to variety; seed pods (not enlarged pistils); long necks; plants potted off-center; traces of sprays or insecticides; dirty pots.

The judges will not consider for judging any single-crowned African violet that has a sucker, any plant that is double-potted or is in a flared-top pot, any plant that shows evidence of pests or disease, or has trimmed leaves. Plants with any of these faults will be *eliminated from consideration.*

AVSA Scale Of Points

All AVSA African violet shows are merit-judged. In other words, each exhibit is judged on its merits rather than one against another. The following Scale of Points is used for judging African violet specimen plants including single-crowned and trailing standard, miniature, and semiminiature varieties:

Symmetry or form	25
Quantity of bloom	25
Condition (cultural perfection)	25
Size and type of blossom	15
Color of blossom	10

The growing and grooming information presented in this book applies to all types of African violets; however, there are additional things to consider in growing and getting the smaller single-crowned ones, trailers and species ready for show.

SEMIMINIATURES AND MINIATURES

AVSA designates two sizes for small-growing African violets: miniatures and semiminiatures. The references and culture pertains to both sizes. Miniatures must be 6" or less in diameter to be entered in the miniatures classes at AVSA Standard Shows; semiminiatures must be 8" or less. The designation for the size of a variety, which is determined by the hybridizer, is found in its description in the *AVML*,

Miniature and semiminiature African violets contend for top awards all over the world. Hybridizers have continually improved them. The result has been freer blooming plants that are less likely to sucker and are available in many different types, with beautiful combinations of foliage and blossom color.

CHOOSING PLANTS: When choosing plants to grow for show, try to select only superior varieties. Look for the plants that have heavy bloom and that the variety blooms true to the hybridizer's description. Choose plants that have overlapping leaves that form a rosette. Some varieties have a more open growth habit and do not have overlapping leaves. These are more challenging to work with.

PROPAGATION: Minis and semis can be propagated using suckers or leaves. Chimeras are only propagated using suckers or blossom stems. Place suckers or leaves in a 3 oz. plastic cup in soilless potting mix; or, you may use a mixture of one part perlite; four parts vermiculite; one-half part fine charcoal, and two parts milled sphagnum moss. Water thoroughly, slip into a plastic baggie and tie closed until plantlets appear on the leaves or the suckers appear to be rooted.

Plastic wrap also works well for providing the necessary humidity while a root system is forming. Use enough plastic wrap to cover the leaf or sucker and part of the pot; then put a rubber band around the plastic under the rim of the pot to secure it. When using plastic wrap, you may need to watch the rooting medium more closely to assure that it doesn't dry out, because the wrap doesn't completely cover the pot.

POTTING: When plantlets are big enough or suckers are well rooted, pot them into 2", 2-1/4", or 2 1/2" plastic pots. African violets have a very fine root system. They need a loose, porous, slightly acid potting mix with good drainage. Do not use a perlite layer in the bottom; they need all of the soil to grow into.

Ideally, miniatures and semiminiature should be repotted every three to six months. Repot plants back into a clean, same-size pot. To do this, carefully remove the plant from its pot, take off all old leaves, which are usually smaller than the new ones, and trim the bottom of the root ball according to the length of the plant's neck. Put a little fresh soil in the bottom of the pot, place the plant in the pot, and add soil to bring the level nearly to the top of the pot. Then water the plant.

The plants should have three to four rows of leaves. Sometimes when repotting you'll end up with one or two rows, but the plant should fill itself out in three or four months. If you end up with one row or just the center, it's going to take up to six months to fill out. It depends on the plant, since some grow a little faster than others.

Some growers repot older plants five months before show with a "hard break"; that is, leaving only two or three layers of leaves and the center crown. This may result in a neck which may require cutting off the lower part of the root ball. The plants will recover quickly. At three months before show, they repot with a "soft break"; removing some outer leaves, if necessary.

WATER: Depending on the conditions in the plant room, top-water once a week. By top watering, there is better control of the plants. Each plant has its own saucer. If excess water remains in the saucers after a half hour, it should be emptied. The temperature in the plant room should stay at around 68 to 70 degrees. The humidity varies from season to season.

FERTILIZER: Use balanced fertilizers such as 14-12-14 or 20-20-20 with the constant feed method using fertilizer at one-quarter to one-eighth strength. Every four to six weeks use plain water.

LIGHTS: Providing the proper amount of light is critical when growing for show. Cultivars differ in the amount of light they need. Plants with dark foliage generally need more light than plants with light or variegated foliage.

Lights should be on a timer ten to twelve hours a day with plants six to twelve inches from the tubes. How closely you place your plants to the light tubes depend on how old the tubes are and on the plants themselves. You need to watch how your plants are reacting to the light and move them to locations under the lights where they do best.

GETTING READY FOR SHOW: Most miniatures and semiminiatures respond very well to disbudding. By disbudding, foliage gaps become less noticeable or disappear when the plant receives adequate light and a balanced diet. Plants are disbudded all the time up to about eight to six weeks before a show. How long you disbud before a show depends on the variety and your growing conditions. Pay attention to how long it takes your plant to come into bloom. Then you will know how to time it in the future. You might think you have your plants figured out, but they don't always cooperate. The outdoor weather and changes of the season can also affect the plants. They seem to know when the weather or season changes even though they are indoors.

Grooming your African violets the week of a show is especially critical. Remove all yellowed or marred leaves unless this drastically upsets the symmetry of the plant. Check your plants very carefully for suckers (growth that shows four leaves but no evidence of a bud). Remove tired-looking or spent blossoms. Most dirt and debris can be removed from the foliage by brushing gently with a soft brush. If your plants are extremely dusty or dirty, give them a bath with tepid water, being careful not to get water on the blossoms. Blot up water drops that remain on the foliage so leaves don't end up water-spotted when you place them back under the lights.

MICRO-MINIATURES

About the time we think there can be nothing new in the growing of African violets, along comes a new twist: miniaturized miniatures. At the 1986 AVSA convention in St. Paul, Minnesota, Holtkamp introduced to the African violet world the first two of its Little Jewel series, 'Little Rose Quartz' and 'Little Sapphire'. Since a miniaturized version of almost anything holds a particular fascination for us, these miniature plants captured the fancy of all conventioneers.

These fascinating little jewels were shown in plastic pots that were perfect 1-1/2" versions of red clay pots with tiny snap-on saucers. The plants were in full bloom and in perfect proportion to the pots.

These miniaturized plants are not bonsai, but some of the techniques of bonsai–such as root restriction and root and foliage pruning–are used. Semiminiature varieties grown in thumb-pots will over grow the pots.

CHARACTERISTICS: Miniature Optimaras have proved to be perfectly adapted to this miniaturizing technique. They probably represent many years of crossbreeding by Holtkamp

WHERE TO GROW THEM: They should be grown in a relatively sheltered draft-free area with stable temperatures and good humidity.

WATERING: If grown in the open, these miniatures need watering every day. The mature plants will survive if an occasional watering day is missed, but will deteriorate if it happens too often.

To avoid the bother of daily watering, individually potted plants may be grown in a terrarium. Under these conditions they need watering about every 5 to 7 days.

LIGHTS: These miniatures need to be as close as 6" to the lights. Semis do well at 8" to 10". Lights should be on for 14 to 16 hours a day.

POTTING: Don't use a layer of perlite in the bottom of the pot; they need all of the soil they can get. Use a soilless potting mix recipe omitting the perlite or remove the larger particles of perlite from a commercial mix.

FERTILIZING: Use a concentration of 1/8 teaspoon to a gallon of water for plants that are watered daily; 1/4 teaspoon to the gallon for terrarium-grown plants. Use fertilizer such as 5-50-17 to discourage rapid growth and to promote maximum bloom.

MAINTENANCE: Potting down the neck on a single-crowned variety requires the delicate skill of microsurgery. You are dealing with a one-inch-deep root ball. The neck should not be more than 1/4" long. Use tweezers for holding the plant and for adding pinches of mix around the neck.

If you are short on patience, use crown-cuttings and start the plant over. This method has to be used with trailers, anyway. With this intricate kind of potting, the pot should be filled to the top with soil mix and then the stub of the crown is pushed down in to the mix.

If you do grow these miniaturized African violets, don't pass up the chance to exhibit them. The amazement of the viewing public will make the effort worthwhile.

TRAILERS

African violet trailers range in size: micro-minis (leaf size approximately 1/4" x 1/2"); miniatures (leaf size approximately 1/2" x 1"); semiminiatures (leaf size approximately 1" x 1-1/2"); and standards (leaf size up to 2").

AVSA Scale of Points for judging trailers is the same as for single-crowned standards and semiminiatures except that trailers are judged on form rather than symmetry.

Refer to the *AVSA Handbook for Growers, Exhibitors, and Judges* for more information.

Miniature And Semiminiature Trailers

Don't be too quick to dismiss a trailer as a so-so performer; they can be deceiving. It may take as long as six months for some of them to show full potential. Start the plantlets in 2" pots and about three months later pot them into 4" pots. Some growers pot the true-trailing miniatures and semiminiatures into 5" or 6" pots in order to grow bigger specimens. If space is limited keep all miniature trailers restricted to 4" pots.

Standard Trailers

The foliage of standard trailers is more flexible to work with but the culture, grooming, and pruning procedures are the same as those for miniatures. Standard trailers may be potted in large shallow saucers or large pan pots. Many standard trailers grow for many years in the same pot without repotting or pruning back, before the long bare stems become evident.

Growing Trailers

PINCHING: Some varieties form numerous multiple crowns naturally and can be left to grow at will. Others need to have the center crown pinched once to encourage formation of extra crowns. Yet others need extensive and continuous pinching in order to achieve full foliage and good form. By observing the growth during the first few months the grower can tell which method is needed for a given variety.

CREATING FORM: Trailers are judged on form rather than symmetry. In order to score highly, the foliage must be full with three or more crowns spaced evenly around the pot. As they progress, some varieties form this desired shape naturally; other varieties must be pruned or staked in order to create good form. When there is a gap in one side of the foliage, one of two moves may correct it. Gradually move a stem into position, staking it in place each time until it stays put. If there is a crown recessed deeply in the gap, pinch out its center so that it will produce multiple crowns and fill in the gap. If a crown spoils the form by jutting out too far, cut it back and follow up by picking off all but one of the new crowns that will form. If this isn't done, the excess crowns again make the plant lopsided.

GROOMING: Most growers observe the usual grooming procedures of washing foliage and removing spent blossoms and marred leaves. But what many new growers fail to recognize is that immature and off-sized leaves must also be removed from trailers. Often what could be perfect trailers go to show looking like porcupines. The leaves should also be all the same size according to their stage of growth from the center of the crowns.

Sometimes one stem of the plant reverts or sports and the leaves are disproportionately large. In this case, the entire crown or stem should be removed. Points would be deducted for this deviation.

REPOTTING TRAILERS: Trailers can be potted down when necks develop. However, in order to exhibit in AVSA shows, the rule is that there shall be only one plant to the pot. The multiple crowns must all emanate from one plant. When a trailer with multiple long necks or stems is potted down, it would no longer be one plant. The stems would be separated by the new soil and each crown might appear to be an independent plant, which could result in the plant being eliminated from consideration for judging. Many growers prefer to have backup plants of the same varieties in various stages of growth. When their trailers get leggy and open, they root crown cuttings and discard the rest of the plant.

However, there is a way to rejuvenate old trailers by repotting. Remove the plant from the pot, cut away the perlite, crumble away most of the soil from the root ball, and trim off excess roots. Prune the top growth leaving enough leaves to manufacture food while the plant is putting out new growth. Scrape the scar tissue from the denuded lower part of the stem. Prepare the pot with fresh perlite and soil mix and repot the plant to the same depth as before. In a few months new crowns will form and the plant will have full foliage and be ready to show off again.

Saintpaulia SPECIES

There are various reasons given as to why growers choose to grow or not to grow and show *Saintpaulia* species plants. There are those who have the 'collection' instinct – they must have one of each in their collection. Others are aware of the possibilities of their extinction in the wild and like the thought of having a bit of history on their plant shelves. Some grow the species because they are a challenge; each one is different. Or, they are seeking variety in their collection.

The other side is that growers shy away from them because of their names. "If I can't pronounce or spell the name I don't want anything to do with it!" Some avoid growing species plants because of their messy blossom dropping habits; they haven't had success in the past; or they expected the species plants to behave as their hybrid cultivars (and they don't!). If you expect a nice symmetrical easy to grow plant, forget the species. But if you want some variety in your growing and are looking for a challenge – go for the 'wild side'!

Selecting Species Show Plants

Select species that are naturally floriferous although some of the species that have rather sparse blooming tendencies have been award winners. The species are listed as having few, some or many blossoms (floriferous) in a quantity of blossom chart in T*he AVSA Handbook for Growers, Exhibitors, and Judges.*

• Select plants that have uniform foliage color throughout and have a good pattern of growth for the particular species.

• Grow the species long enough to know its growth characteristics and the environmental conditions in which it grows best.

• Observe your species plants regularly. You might be surprised to find a specimen that has "done its own thing" right there on your plant shelf and is an excellent candidate for a show entry.

AVSA Scale Of Points For Species

All species should be entered in the class designated for species in an AVSA show. However, trailing species plants in the class for species or from AVSA collections, may be considered for Best Trailer.

The following AVSA Scale of Points is used for judging species:

Cultural perfection	50 points
Grooming	30 points
Quantity of bloom (according to species).	20 points

CULTURAL PERFECTION accounts for half of the points in judging species plants. For species, cultural perfection is how well the plant is grown given its genetic potential. You can obtain cultural perfection with species plants using the same horticultural practices that you use for all African violets: frequent repotting, routine fertilizing, uniform watering, proper lighting. It takes some experimenting to find the best conditions in your environment for each of the species.

STEPS TO CULTURAL PERFECTION:

- Consistent care: watering, fertilizer, repotting, lighting. Not all of the species have the same needs for light and water.

- Species plants have smaller root systems than the modern hybrids and like a very light, porous soil, especially if wick watered.

- Pot size: The 1:3 ratio of rosette plants (p. 88) is not the criteria for most of the species. Pot size should be in proportion to the plant and with proportion that looks balanced. (The 1:3 ratio has been so emphasized that it is difficult to diverge.) Like all African violets, the species plants need to be root bound to bloom. Because of the shallow root systems, shallow pan pots are a good choice.

- Poor shape or form is considered under culture and may lead to loss of points, but symmetry or lack of it is up to the plant to decide. Each species has its own characteristic form. Wayward growth habits that lead to poor shape or form is the tendency of some species. It is often possible to improve the shape of a plant by removing wayward side shoots and errant leaves

- Trailing forms do not have to have multiple crowns. Suckers on usually single crowned plants are acceptable (back to that *native or wild* habit of species).

- *The Handbook* states: "we should exhibit them as they are, without artificially pruning them to meet certain criteria."

GROOMING species plants means keeping the spent blossoms, stems, and yellowed leaves removed. Grooming species plants follow the same guidelines as grooming all of your African violets–anything that will improve the appearance of the plant.

QUANTITY OF BLOOM differs considerably with species. A list of all of the species according to their *tendency* toward blooming is included in the *Handbook;* however, many factors in the growing conditions may intervene so that for one person, a particular species blooms freely while for another, that same species may not ever bloom.

CHECK-LIST: WHAT THE JUDGES LOOK FOR IN A SHOW PLANT

SYMMETRY .... 25 Points*
    Is the foliage symmetrical?... _____
    Does it have good form if it is a trailer?.. _____
    Are there gaps between leaves? Can this be improved? .... _____
    Do the petioles come straight out from the stem?......................... _____
    Do the leaves overlap leaving a rosette form? .... _____

CONDITION (cultural perfection) .... 25 Points
    Is the plant mature? (Would it be a better show plant next year?).... _____
    Are there signs of insect damage or disease? .... _____
    Are there any suckers or parts of suckers? .... _____
    Is the plant centered in the pot?.. _____
    Is the plant over or under potted?... _____
    Is there a neck? .... _____
    Is there an open pattern with soil showing excessively?.............. _____
    Is there evidence of a culture break, i.e., evidence of an interrupted
        growth pattern (small inner row of leaves)?........................... _____
    Are there any baby leaves – smaller leaves below large leaves? ... _____
    Has all soil, dust, and spray residue on leaves or petioles been removed? ..... _____
    Have all spent or damaged blossoms been removed? .... _____
    Have all damaged leaves been removed? (If a damaged leaf affects
        symmetry, consider the option of leaving it vs. removing it.)..... _____
    Have all petiole, peduncle and/or pedicel stubs been removed?...... _____
    Have all leaf supports or guides been removed?........................... _____
    Is the pot clean?... _____

QUANTITY OF BLOOM (Number according to variety and type) ..... 25 Points
    Standard mature plant – 20 to 25.. _____
    Small standard plant (8" to 10") – 10 to 15 .... _____
    Semiminiatures – 10 to 20... _____
    Miniatures – 6 to 12... _____
    Trailers - Plant has at least three crowns..................................... _____
        Blossoms on all crowns.. _____

SIZE AND TYPE OF BLOSSOM (Compare with descriptions in *AVML*) .... 15 Points
    Blossoms are the size according to the variety............................. _____
    Blossoms are the type according to the variety .... _____

COLOR OF BLOSSOM .... 10 Points
    Color according to description .... _____
    Solid color among multicolor and vice versa removed.................. _____

*See the AVSA Scale of Points (p. 82) and the *AVSA Handbook for Growers, Exhibitors, and Judges* for more information..

Pre-Show Planning

About three months before a show, the critical timing for final plant growth and inducing floriferousness begins. These steps *cannot* be taken at the grower's convenience. If plants are to be at their peak condition by show time, the procedures must be implemented at the proper times. The weekly sequence should be recorded on a calendar so that the grower will be reminded to check the pre-show schedule and follow the recommendations given in this chapter.

The grower walks a cultural tightrope in the months before a show; the methods used to increase growth and blossoming must be carefully balanced against the risk of spoiling symmetry by creating off-sized rows of leaves or burning or spotting sensitive foliage.

JANUARY

sun	mon	tues	wed	thurs	fri	sat
			1	2	3	4 *12 weeks to show*
5	6	7	8	9	10	11
12	13	14	15 *AVC-SC luncheon*	16 *VC-AVS meeting*	17	18 *10 weeks to show*
19	20	21	22	23	24	25
26	27	28	29	30	31	*8 weeks to show*

PRE-SHOW SCHEDULE:

Count back from the show date and mark the dates on the calendar for twelve weeks before the show, ten weeks before, etc., down to one week and one day!

12 WEEKS: Remove leaves. Re-pot; pot down if there are necks or pot up. If you choose to do it, foliar feed once in addition to regular fertilizing. Lights should be on twelve hours a day.

10 WEEKS: Completely disbud all plants except perhaps miniatures and trailers. Put one new tube in each fixture. Start bloom-booster (5-57-17, 20-60-20) fertilizer formula.

9 WEEKS: Increase light time by one hour to thirteen hours. *Disbud heavily variegated varieties and double varieties for the last time.* Continue to disbud all other varieties. Continue bloom-booster fertilizer.

8 WEEKS: Increase light time by one hour. Disbud doubles and lightly variegated varieties for the last time. Continue to disbud semidouble stars and singles. Check for suckers. Continue bloom-booster. Foliar feed once more (optional).

7 WEEKS: Increase light time by one hour (to fifteen hours). *Disbud semidouble stars for the last time.* Change to 12-36-14 or 15-30-15 fertilizer formula for the remaining weeks.

6 WEEKS: *Disbud singles for the last time.* Check for suckers. Wash foliage.

1 WEEK: Remove spent blossoms, peduncles, and pedicel stubs. Check for suckers. Brush away soil particles, etc. Pot down necks or pot up only if necessary. (See Last Minute Potting Tips, p. 93.)

1 DAY: Again remove spent blossoms, etc. Remove leaf support rings. Place plants in transporting boxes so that the foliage is supported.

At sixteen weeks (3 months) before show, pot up large standards already show size; let bloom once (one or two blossom stalks) after re-potting, then begin disbudding. Fertilize with a balanced fertilizer. At twelve weeks, pot up smaller standards moving up to show size. Let bloom once after re-potting and then begin disbudding. At this time, foliage should be washed. When it is fresh and dust-free, it will be able to put out the energy required for the new growth that will be activated by the potting procedures. Double check for the presence of pests, particularly the more common ones such as thrips and cyclamen mites. If they are discovered at this time, they can be eliminated without damaging show plants and future blossoms. Try to avoid bringing any new plants into your collection during the next three months.

Apply the following procedures during the designated weeks of the pre-show schedule.

Final Potting

After repotting, growth slows down temporarily as the root system expands into the new soil. Only then can energy be expended for new growth and production of blossoms. Any marred, immature, or off-size leaves remaining in the outer row should be removed. If necessary, remove the entire outer row. Even if the outer row is perfect, the grower may decide to remove it in order to restrict the plant size.

At this point, the grower decides what size pot to use for each plant. The pot size is determined by the diameter of the existing foliage and by estimating the growth rate for the next three months.

Potting down: A mature plant that is now growing in a five-inch pot and is to be potted down into the same-sized pot will have a growth rate of about one inch a month for the next few months (depending on the variety).

Potting up: If a plant is potted up to the next size pot, the growth rate will be about three inches the first month and about one inch a month for the next few months.

Pot-To-Foliage Proportion

In choosing the pot size, the rule of thumb is that the foliage should be approximately three times wider, leaf-tip-to-leaf-tip, than the diameter of the pot. (This is commonly referred to as the 1:3 ratio). Example: a fifteen-inch plant takes a five-inch pot. This is only a guideline; it is impossible to achieve these exact measurements. Judges do not measure foliage; they rely on their training and good judgment to determine whether the pot is in pleasing proportion to the amount of foliage. (Tall pots show up a discrepancy in proportion more readily than do shallow pots.)

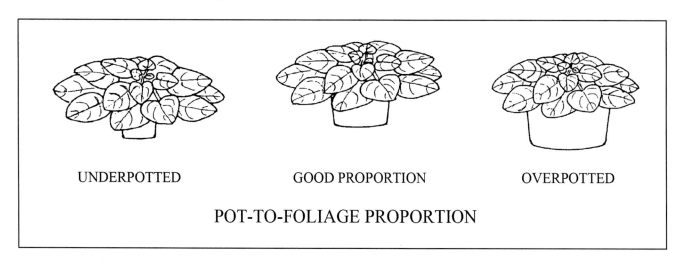

UNDERPOTTED   GOOD PROPORTION   OVERPOTTED

POT-TO-FOLIAGE PROPORTION

Fertilizing Program

A bloom-booster is used during the eighth, ninth, and tenth weeks before show to encourage maximum setting of buds. A bloom-booster is any fertilizer formula in which about 70% of the total formula is phosphorus, the element that most affects blooming. For example: 5-50-17, 12-55-6. (The regular formulas of 12-36-14, 15-30-15, 20-20-20 add up to 60%.)

Bloom-boosters are low in nitrogen, so they are used only long enough to produce extra bloom. After that, a more balanced fertilizer is resumed to lessen the chance that off-sized leaves will form. Many experienced show growers do not use bloom-booster; they depend on decreasing the light distance and increasing the light hours to achieve full blossom count at show time, but this requires careful observation of their plants.

Foliar feeding, if used, is spaced out in the pre-show schedule to give a boost to root formation after repotting and as an additional boost for blossoms eight weeks before the show. Follow Foliar Feeding directions in the section on Fertilizing, p. 48.

Light-Hour Changes

Starting nine weeks before the show, light hours are increased gradually to speed up growth. Blossoms are produced only on new growth. Since plants assimilate nutrients during the light hours, increased light hours mean increased assimilation of nutrients and, therefore, increased growth. The light hours are increased one hour a week over a three-week period. This gradual change allows foliage to adapt to the increased light without burning or altering the foliage pattern.

Many experienced show growers follow variations to the show calendar in timing their show plants; most variations require careful observation of their plants.

Final Disbudding

The timing for full floriferousness varies according to weather conditions, cultural practices, and variety characteristics. For example, a period of hot weather speeds up blooming and a period of cold weather slows it down. If a lapse in cultural practices occurs (allowing plants to go dry, for example), growth is slowed, and timing for floriferousness will be off schedule. Heavily variegated varieties take longer to come into bloom than lightly variegated ones; the reduced areas of chlorophyll in the foliage mean a slower growth rate for the plant. Some double-blossomed plants take longer than other doubles to come into full bloom. The type of fluorescent tubes used and distance from the tubes are also factors (See Fluorescent Tube Types, p.29).

The recommended disbudding schedule in this chapter is based on the following considerations:

1. Maintaining the normal temperature range of 65°F to 75°F.

2. Maintaining a humidity of 50% to 60%.

3. Using Standard Gro-Lux fluorescent tubes. Other types or combinations of fluorescent tubes may require different timing.

Blossom Check

Two or three weeks before show, remove blossoms that have opened too early for the show. Do this by cutting the pedicel (the small stalk supporting each flower). Usually this will be the first flower of a cluster and it will begin to fade by show time. Removing this blossom will allow the others to develop to the same size. The first flower of a cluster uses all of the plants energy, causing the later blooms to be smaller.

The center foliage in some plants may be so dense that the blossom stalks have a difficult time emerging above the leaves. Carefully and gently bring any blossom stalks that are hiding under the foliage up from under leaves.

Controlling Blooming Time

Temperature control can be used with some degree of effectiveness in speeding up or slowing down blooming. In the final weeks before show, increasing the daytime temperature to 80°F and keeping nighttime temperature at 70°F can speed up blooming. If blossoms are opening too soon, keep daytime temperature at 70°F and nighttime temperature at about 60°F.

If at three weeks before show, there aren't quite a few open blossoms, there are some things to do to speed up the blooming: raise the temperature in the growing area, place the plants on top shelves, add one hour of light, and lower the fixtures so the lights are closer to the plants.

If the plants are completely in bloom two weeks before the show, lower the temperature, place the plants at the bottom of the light stand where it is cooler, and place them farther from the light source by raising the fixtures or putting them at the side of the stand.

It takes years of experience to recognize whether the majority of the blossoms are opening too soon or not soon enough; new growers should not aggravate themselves by playing this guessing game. Follow the recommended disbudding schedule and try to maintain the normal temperature range. This way at least 80% of the plants will probably bloom on schedule.

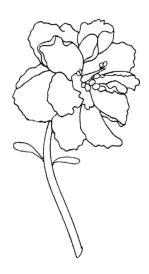

SELECTING ENTRIES

No one wants to box and transport less than blue-ribbon plants to a show, but new growers often judge their own plants so severely that they end up not taking any plants at all.

Even experienced growers can develop a bad case of the doubts. The phrase "I have better looking plants than *those* at home" has become a standing joke among exhibitors as they view the entries in a show. Since African violets left on the shelves never win awards, the question is this: How can you impartially judge your own plants?

Classification chairpersons sometimes ask for a pre-entry list as much as a month in advance of the show (See Keeping Records, p. 19). It is difficult to predict which plants will have the proper amount of blossoms, so the grower must list almost every plant in his collection. Clearly, the time to judge your own plants is a few days before the show when you are checking your copy of the pre-entry sheet to see which plants should be deleted.

Evaluate each plant while you are looking at the AVSA Scale of Points and the judging guidelines. Mentally deduct points for lack of perfection under each part of the scale. New growers should then go back and add as many as ten points to the score of each plant; seasoned show growers should add up to five points. These are the ranges by which most growers tend to underestimate the quality of their plants.

The next step is to choose a collection of three registered varieties as entries in the AVSA Collection class. (These are the only entries that are required to be registered varieties.) Next to the Best in Show award, the AVSA Collection Awards are the most prestigious in the show.

AVSA COLLECTION CLASS

A collection class is composed of three different registered varieties, all of the same type and size designation. It must be three single-crowned or trailing standards, three miniatures, three semi-miniatures, or three species. Each plant in the collection is point-scored individually and the scores are totaled to determine first place (gold rosette) and second place (purple rosette). If there is a tie, the judges re-evaluate the two collections.

From the plants which you believe are blue-ribbon quality, line up on your floor only those that are registered and point score each plant. Consider removing support rings if you want to see how well the petioles hold up. At this point, most growers are fortunate to have three high-scoring plants of one type (standard single-crowned, etc.). The first inclination of the new grower is to choose a "matched set" (all variegated or all plain, all the same-sized plant, all pink blossoms, etc.).

Experienced growers who have a wall full of AVSA gold rosettes can afford to give themselves the extra challenge of trying for a matched set. The inclination of the new grower is to choose the most colorfully flamboyant varieties, but it is best to stop and point-score; plainer varieties should be chosen if they are likely to score higher.

The fact that a collection is a matched set makes no difference in the judging; each plant is judged individually.

New growers often feel intimidated when entering the collection class, because they are competing against top growers; but they should remember that it costs them nothing to enter. The plants receive the ribbons to which they are entitled, they are eligible for all other special awards, and blue ribbons count toward sweepstakes.

This is usually the first class the judges check when they are looking for the best specimen plant in the show. And keep this in mind: you will never win a collection award unless you enter plants in that class.

SHOW SCHEDULE

Every AVSA Standard Show must have an approved show schedule that conforms to AVSA requirements; it should be available early for the committees, members and exhibitors, and judges. The schedule includes the rules and regulations for the show and the classes that will be included.

The schedule is the law of the show.

Classes are divided according to blossom color and type (solid colors, two-toned, multicolor, edged, fantasy, and chimera), foliage (plain and variegated), and by plant size and type (standard, miniature, semiminiature, trailers, species, and new cultivars). *The Handbook for Growers, Exhibitors, and Judges* includes all of the guidelines for an affiliate show, including a sample show schedule.

The show schedule is useful when growers are selecting entries and preparing exhibits for the show. Here are some of the guidelines that every exhibitor must conform to:

- *All African violet species, cultivars, and other gesneriads shall be correctly named.* It is important to keep all plants labeled correctly. A cultivar does not have to be listed in the *African Violet Master List* to be entered in a show; it may be a new variety that has not been listed or an older variety that was never listed.

- *All African violet exhibits must be in bloom.*

- *All African violet exhibits, except trailers and species, must be single-crowned plants. (No suckers!)*

- *Plants may be slip-potted into clean, non-decorative pots.* Show rules may dictate the color of the pot; it usually must be the same color as the pot underneath. Slip-potting is not the same as "double-potting."

- *Any number of plants may be entered in each class by an exhibitor, but an exhibitor may not enter more than one plant of a variety in the same class.*

- *The schedule must include the hours, days, month and year of the show,* and the rules will tell the exhibitors when they may enter their plants.

- *All plants must have been in the possession of their exhibitors for at least three months before exhibiting in a show.*

An exhibitor may facilitate the entries process by listing all plants being entered by variety name, class number (from the schedule), and if entering an AVSA Collection Class, the registration number. (Refer to *First Class* or the *AVML* for this information.)

Last Minute Show Preparation

POTTING

A week–or even a few days before a show–the plants will need to be checked to see if any last minute repotting should be done. Repotting at this stage is tricky and the risks are high. New growers may not be confident enough of their potting skills to try it, but many experienced growers practice it routinely.

UNDERPOTTED PLANTS: If some of the best plants (particularly those chosen for the AVSA Collection) are noticeably under-potted, they should be potted up to the next size pot. The mold-potting technique is used except that the inner pot is placed the full depth of the larger pot instead of on top of the perlite layer. This procedure is used because the plant is transferred with the root ball, including the perlite layer, intact. It is better to avoid disturbing the roots. The proper depth of perlite and soil mix is added around the inner pot and pressed down firmly. Before adding the soil, saturate the perlite layer with water so that it will hold its shape when the inner pot is removed. Remove the inner pot, transfer the plant carefully into the prepared hole, and press the root ball firmly into place.

This last-minute potting procedure may also be used for those large-growing varieties that have been grown in 4" or 5" pots in order to restrict their size. At show time the foliage is only about 18" in diameter instead of 22" or so. They are then potted up to 6" pots just before the show. After the show, they can be potted back down again.

Note: This must be done "at the last minute." Doing this two or three weeks before the show will slow down the opening of blossoms; the plant's energy will go into growing roots into the new potting mix.

PLANTS WITH NECKS: If you have misjudged and a row of leaves must be removed, the resulting neck will be only about 1/4" long. In this case, soil mix can be added to the pot and leveled off around the neck. If the plant has been potted at the right depth (3/4" free space at the top of the pot), there will be 1/2" of free space remaining.

However, if this has already been done and still more leaves must be removed, the neck will then be too long to add more soil and the plant must be potted down. *Do not mound soil around the neck in an attempt to disguise it!* The judges will not be fooled and points will be deducted. Not only that, but the petioles will not rest straight across the rim of the pot causing the petioles to sag and possibly ruining symmetry.

93

Lift the plant out of the pot and cut away enough of the perlite layer to equal the length of the neck. Place the plant back in the same pot without adding any new perlite. This will lower the plant sufficiently in the pot without cutting into the soil part of the root ball. Add new soil around the neck. After the show, the plant can be properly repotted.

SLIP POTTING:

Slip potting with a moisture barrier (often a requirement in show rules) may not be a requirement in your show schedule, but has tremendous advantages. To slip pot you use either the same size pot or one that is only *very slightly* larger, line it with plastic, and *slip the pot* containing the plant into the plastic lined pot. This helps keep the plant moist, will protect the plant from any creepy crawlers that are on the tabletops, and protects the table covering from soil particles and water leakage. Check the show schedule for rules regarding color of outside pots.

LAST MINUTE GROOMING

The day before the show the plants must be groomed to the most minute detail. Don't risk losing even a fraction of a point for overlooked peduncle or pedicel stubs, spent blossoms, or soil particles on the leaves. Look particularly close for suckers that may have been over-looked. They seem to jump up overnight.

A small soft brush, a piece of natural sponge, and a container of dilute vinegar water (1/2 teaspoon vinegar to 1 cup water) is useful when doing the final grooming just before entries. Water spots and white crust on the edges of leaves can occur during transport. The dilute vinegar water or a broken petiole off a discarded leaf can be used to remove most of these spots.

Some exhibitors, in a desperate attempt to have as much bloom as possible, leave one or two blossoms attached to an already denuded peduncle. Judges wince when they see these. Another motive for leaving these stragglers is achieve the even spacing of blossoms around the crown. Don't do it! It is better to lose the

points than to offend the sensibilities of the judges and viewers.

BOXING SHOW PLANTS

If it is a large show with many exhibitors, make your boxes easy to identify by decorating them with bright strips of tape or press-on paper. Print your name all the way around the edge of the box in bold print.

Growers who live in areas of the country where the weather is less than ideal–or if the show is many hours distant–should box their plants in closed containers. Large, long commercial flower shipping boxes will hold several large plants. A deep layer of shredded newspaper will cushion the foliage and the plants will arrive in excellent condition.

There are many types and sizes of plastic containers that are excellent for transporting plants to show. Most are made to stack and the rigid construction protects the plants.

Foam rubber or styrofoam can be cut to the dimensions of the container bottom. Then for pot-sized holes can be cut in the foam for each specific size pot. Cardboard flats (from grocery or convenience stores) measure about 10-1/2" by 15-1/2" by 3" deep can also be cut to support pots and will fit inside plastic or cardboard boxes. This will keep the plants from shifting.

Tissue paper, plastic grocery bags, or shredded paper will add support under the leaves. Be sure to secure the lids of the containers with bungee cord, strap or tape.

TRANSPORTING PLANTS TO SHOW

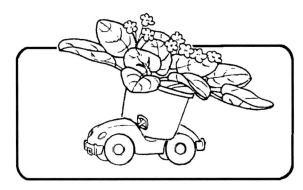

Someone once remarked that pianos are easier to move than plants. You soon learn the truth of that observation the first time you try to get African violets to a judged show in good condition.

Stackable plastic containers or heavy cardboard boxes should be packed so that there is no shifting if an unavoidable slamming on of brakes occurs; otherwise, plants that started the trip in the back seat can wind up in the front seat.

Commercial carriers generate their share of problems. Boxes marked on each side with big red arrows and lettered, "This Side Up" are turned upside down by airline loading personnel or helpful cab drivers. All you can do is choose the best packing method for your situation and hope for the best.

If you live in a temperate climate and don't have far to drive, an open-box carrier works well for transporting plants to show. The pots should sit deeply enough in the box so that the leaves are supported.

When transporting plants in a vehicle such as a station wagon with an expanse of windows, the plants have to be protected from the direct sun. Travel in the early morning or evening or tape newspapers over the side windows of untinted glass.

ARE YOU READY TO GO TO SHOW?

Are boxes ready to transport plants to show? .... ____

Are the plants "slip potted" with a moisture barrier? .... ____

Is there an identifying label on the inner pots? .... ____

Are the plants spotlessly clean? .... ____

Are all leaf supports removed? (You may choose to leave leaf supports on
    to transport but don't forget to remove them before entries) .... ____

Do you have a list of all of your show plants? .... ____

Do you have the classification numbers from the schedule on your list? .... ____

Do you have a grooming kit with brushes, scissors, long tweezers, sponge,
    distilled water with vinegar, etc. for last minute grooming? .... ____

Do you have extra pots (all sizes), a baggie with dry soil (in case you have a
    mishap), a spray bottle with distilled water ready to go? .... ____

Have you done a last minute check of all the items on the Checklist, page 86? ____

LET'S GO TO THE SHOW!

At The Show

FINAL GROOMING

When you arrive at the show with your plants, locate the grooming area in the entries and classification room. Unpack your plants at a designated table where you can do the final grooming.

Check the placement of foliage as you do the final grooming. The leaves may be out of position from the handling. The foliage should be arranged so that the leaves of each row are in the proper over-lapping position. This is particularly important for the plants entered in the AVSA Collection class.

Once you are satisfied that you have done all that you can to make your plants more perfect (no dust particles, wilting blossoms, water spots, last check for suckers), you will take your prepared list of plants to the classification chairman who will check your plants against their descriptions and assign them to appropriate classes according to the show schedule. The entries committee will print labels for your plants and give them to you on stakes for you to place in the pots with your plants. Once you have placed the stakes and given your plants one last minute check, the placement committee will take over. (Don't ever let yourself hear someone comment that your plant would have been on the honor table if it hadn't had specks of dirt on the foliage!) This is the last you will see your plants until you view them on the show table after judging is over and the show room is open for viewing.

> An award-winning African violet isn't just grown–it is created.
> A Best in Show Winner

SHOW MANNERS

Competition brings out the worst in some people and the best in others. Make sure you place yourself in the latter category. You will have much more fun exhibiting if you observe two simple rules of good show manners. First, always do your share of the work. New growers may not be aware of how many months of preparation go into putting on a judged show. To arrive at the last minute, enter your plants, return to pick them up (plus possible awards), and go home will not win friends and influence people. The show chairman can always find a job for even the most inexperienced club member. Ask.

Second, be delighted if you win, but also be a good loser. Even though you may pride your self on being a good sport, there may come a time when you are tempted to challenge a judging decision you believe to be unfair. Should that day come, bite your tongue! Creating a big stir puts you in an unflattering light and probably won't change a thing. (The decision of the judges is final.) As an exhibitor, you can't know of all the factors that went into making a decision. For the most part, judges are very conscientious and make every effort to be fair. Shrug off the defeat and be the first to congratulate the winners.

And finally, keep in mind that everyone is under pressure: the show committee, the judges, and the exhibitors. Put all of your competitive drive into the growing of plants. After they are entered in a show, relax, have fun, and consider any awards you win as a bonus for an exciting experience.

After the Show

With the possible exception of growers who are taking home a highly satisfactory number of ribbons, there will probably be a little letdown when the show is over. Before you start packing up, spend a few minutes looking around and being aware of what has taken place. Compliments to the show committee might be in order, and some camaraderie with your fellow growers can help to make everyone look forward with pleasure to the next year.

PEST PRECAUTIONS

Every time plants are exhibited in a show, there is a chance that a stray pest or two will be brought home. It is well worth the time to take precautions instead of discovering thrips or cyclamen mites a month or two later.

If possible, disbud the plants before they leave the showroom. If not, after the plants have been brought into the house, remove the outside slip pot and completely disbud them before taking them into the plant room.

The most important thing: Until you are reasonably sure that no pests have hitched a ride, do your best to keep the returning show plants from being anywhere near the plants that stayed at home. Preventive applications of pesticides are not usually recommended, but if you have reason to believe that there were plants on the show or sales tables with signs of mites or thrips, take preventive action (See, p.102).

REJUVENATING SHOW PLANTS

After the *grower* recovers from the show, the plants will need further attention. They have been pushed to their peak of perfection for exhibition; now they need to be refreshed and given a new start. The first step in the rejuvenating process is disbudding. Disbudding is not only a pest prevention step but it also allows the center

of the plant to recover from the effects of heavy blooming. The younger center leaves regain their shape and new leaves start forming.

The next step is to wash the foliage so that the plants have a fresh start in preparation for the next cycle. In the following weeks, thin out the collection, groom and remove leaves, and repot where necessary.

Reduce light hours by one hour a week until the normal schedule is reached.

REDUCING THE COLLECTION

Just before a show is usually the time of the year when the shelves are overflowing with plants. New varieties have matured and are ready for exhibition; older varieties have been grown to their maximum size. When the show is over, it is time to evaluate all the plants and determine which ones should be eliminated from your collection. The remaining plants will have breathing room and new varieties can be added.

It is surprising how easy it is to spot the ones that should no longer be given shelf space. We look at our plants every day, but we don't really see them until it is time to make these decisions.

Good homes need to be found for these that are not really show quality; only the most calloused of growers can relegate them to the trashcan. Take a chance. Pass them on to someone else and make room for the fun of the hunt for new ones. Every grower believes that the next plant will be that rare, perfect show plant that will create a sensation at the next show.

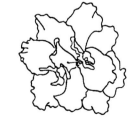

STORING SHOW PLANTS

Part of the fun of growing show plants is the never-ending search for a new, perfect variety. The picking and choosing from nursery stock, club plant sales, catalogs, and *African Violet Magazine* advertisements is exquisite agony. Anyone who has ever shopped through mail order catalogs knows the feeling–a limited budget (in most cases, limited space) and hundreds of tempting items from which to choose.

Even though you may keep only one of the new varieties for your collection, all of them must be grown to about 10" size in order to determine their potential show quality. And so, when you think of the logistics of adding ten or more new plants to two light stands that are already full of plants, then you know something has to give. There will always be some varieties that are expendable, but there will be favorite show plants that you will never want to give up. Also when you find yourself entering the same sure winners each year it gets boring and you know you are not really challenging yourself. This is the time to consider temporarily retiring some of the older varieties.

Don't take the chance of putting down a leaf in order to save the variety for future growing. Just as some children may be parental look-a-likes, others are so different that their parentage is questioned. So it is with the progeny of leaf cuttings. Keeping a leaf of a good show plant for leaf cuttings can produce weak and insignificant plants in comparison to the magnificence of the original plant.

Therefore, you should never give up a perfect show variety; always store the original genetic material in the form of the crown. Even this method is not a 100% guarantee, but it does provide the best odds. Many varieties are unstable and may revert regardless of what you do. Even though revert is a commonly used term, plants do not actually revert, but rather they sport. The sport may have different characteristics from either the parents or the hybrid.

Following the procedures described below, a large number of standard-sized varieties can be stored on one 14" x 18" cafeteria tray for as long as three years.

Storage Procedures:

1. Break the foliage down to just the three center leaves.

2. Cut the main stem of the plant to 1-1/2" below the crown. Scrape the stub to remove any old scar tissue (from previously removed leaves) and to remove the remnants of the petioles just removed. Do not add rooting powder. The object is to retard growth.

3. Place the stub in moist leaf start mix in a 2" pot (3 oz. plastic drinking cups work well for this purpose). If you use the cups, do not put holes in the bottom of them. Do not bag or cover the plants with plastic.

4. About every five to seven days, add just enough water (use the regular fertilizer solution) to the mix to keep it *barely* damp.

5. These plants are to be kept under lights but not necessarily prime light. Place in the miscellaneous area of leaf cuttings and plantlets.

The crown will atrophy and the leaves will take on a leathery texture. If the stub is kept on the dry side, it will neither grow nor bloom. All that matters is that a spark of life is maintained. When you are ready to bring a plant out of hibernation:

1. Lightly water it for the first couple days. (It may be necessary to cut a hole in the bottom of the plastic cup for drainage.) Place the plant in a covered container.

Within a week, the stem should have stiffened and photosynthesis should be occurring again. The plant should remain in the closed environment for at least two more weeks to allow the roots to regenerate.

2. At the end of this two to three week period, repot the crown in fresh soil mix and treat like any other plant of similar size.

In four to six months it should be back to show plant size.

Vacations

The casual grower has many options for preparing African violets to survive a vacation. The methods range from bagging or wicking to putting them in the bathtub on wet newspapers. Under natural light the self-watering pots allow the casual grower to take up to a ten-day vacation.

The commercially available 11" x 21" trays with egg crating will hold nearly two quarts of water and last at least 2 weeks. The plant sitter just pours more water in the trays if needed.

For dedicated show plant growers, the options narrow. It is either stay home or train a plant sitter. Most of us quickly rule out staying home; there's no fun in that. Training a plant sitter is easier than you may think. Whether your plant sitter is an experienced grower or has a brown thumb, be sure they watch you water your plants at least once before they take responsibility.

Always write out detailed instructions outlining when to water, what is to be watered and what is not to be watered, and if the saucers need to be emptied the next day. Tape a note to each plant or group of plants (don't rely on post-its to stay stuck). It is easier to read a taped note that says "add 1/2" water to each saucer on this shelf" than to try to figure that out from a sheet of instructions.

If possible have the fertilized water ready to use so it does not have to be mixed by the sitter. Be sure to reward your sitter with a like favor or a thank you gift – it's a big job.

Prepare trays of plantlets, leaf cuttings, miniatures, etc. by disbudding and watering them. Use large sheets of lightweight plastic and completely cover the trays tucking the plastic under all edges to create an almost airtight tent. If the plant room doesn't get too hot, these plants keep nicely under the lights for up to three weeks.

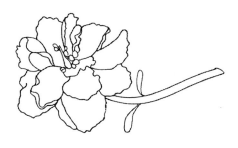

Cross-Country Moving

The prospect of a long-distance move makes the heart of an African violet grower sink. The logistics of packing and moving dozens of environmentally fragile plants is mind-boggling. Restaurant stops have to be chosen carefully so that the car can be parked in the shade and plant boxes must be hauled into motel rooms at night. This is a good way to bring on nervous breakdowns and split up families!

The easiest, safest, and sanest way to move African violets is to apply the same method as used in storing show plants. After the crowns have been potted, roll a half-sheet of newspaper around the pot and fold over the excess at the top and bottom and tape or staple it down. These bundles can be packed in a box in an upright position and will survive for many days on the road without attention. After arriving at the destination, they will keep for many weeks (or even months) until you are ready to pot again.

By following this procedure, you are doing at your convenience what you would probably have to do in the end if you tried to move the plants intact.

Since this book was written in 1985, numerous new pesticides, insecticides, and fungicides have been made available for agricultural, greenhouse and nursery use and many more are being developed for a wide variety of insect and mite pests. Also, a number of older products have been taken off the market for environmental and safety reasons. Many of the newer products are not suitable for in-home use; however, several new products may effectively be used on African violets. See Pesticide Arsenal, p. 111, for information on several of these products.

CHEMICALS: TOXIC or SAFE?

Recently, several commonly used insecticides were removed from sale by the Environmental Protection Agency (EPA); others products are being phased out due to safety concerns. Some of these products may be in your cupboards.

Many of the older chemicals are toxic, readily absorbed through the skin and mucous membranes, and may be dangerous to your health. Highly toxic chemicals are available only to licensed handlers, but no one really knows what the long-term, accumulative effects of the so-called "safe" chemicals are.

Commercial nurseries have no choice but to employ preventive programs; one outbreak of a pest or disease and they are out of business for weeks or perhaps months. Nurserymen have been trained in the proper use of pesticides and they have to pass rigid testing in order to get a license to use highly toxic chemicals.

Homeowner products should have the pest or a similar pest name on the container and come in ready to use sprays, dusts, or liquids that are sold at garden centers. Always be sure that the pesticide label is for in-home (*interiorscape*) use. Many of the newer products are not toxic to humans and mammals but are toxic to fish and amphibians and to beneficial insects such

as bees. Use all products according to label directions and dispose of unused pesticides during local toxic waste collection days in your community.

"Two years of thrips is long enough."

Read the specimen label for any pesticide and its associated Material Safety Data Sheet (MSDS), both available on-line (See Pesticides). The MSDS includes a lot of information, but the most useful are first aid, toxicological and ecological information. The specimen label will describe the precautions to be used in applying the chemical and to minimize the possible development of resistance in the target pest. These recommendations include rotating chemicals and implementing an integrated pest management program (using a wide range of mechanical, biological, chemical, and other preventive and treatment methods to manage potential pest problems).

Entomologists warn us that insects can build up a tolerance to pesticides and can develop mutant strains that are resistant to existing ones. This is more likely to happen when chemicals are used by amateurs in ineffectual amounts or with improper techniques and procedures. When a pest does show up in your collection, shoot to kill. Determine the proper chemical and dosage to be used, carefully follow directions, and take all precautions. Wear a mask, long-sleeved shirt, and gloves. Afterward, do a thorough washing of skin, clothes, and equipment.

Methods of applying chemicals to plants include sprays, drenches, and systemics.

SPRAYS: Sprays should be mixed according to label directions and should be mixed fresh for each application. Spray only after the room temperature reaches 70-75°F. Spray early in the day so that plants are completely dry before the temperature starts to drop in the evening. It is not necessary to turn off fluorescent lights during or after spraying.

SYSTEMICS AND DRENCHES: Don't add systemics to soil mix or use a chemical drench on plants unless given specific instructions to do so. Many warnings have been published against handling soil mix or plant tissue that has been treated with chemicals. It just isn't practical to wear gloves and a mask when potting plants or handling leaves.

Systemic insecticides are those in which the active ingredient is taken up by the plant roots and transported to locations throughout the plant, such as growing points, where it can affect plant-feeding pests. The water solubility of systemic insecticides determines their movement within plants and they are subject to leaching.

A new group of insecticide/miticides now on the market have *translaminar*, or local, systemic activity. These chemicals penetrate leaf tissue and form a reservoir of the active ingredient within the leaf. This provides residual activity against certain foliar-feeding insects and mites. These products are applied as a spray.

Sprays designated as safe for African violets will not damage foliage if used in the recommended amounts, but chemical drenches are another matter. Although African violets will survive drenches of pesticides or fungicides, mixtures strong enough to kill pests or pathogens are detrimental to the roots, and thus the foliage.

PREVENTION

Preventive application of pesticides is not recommended; however, many growers choose to follow a preventive regimen of chemical treatment for all in-coming plants. The cost involved, wasting the compound, and unnecessary exposure are compelling reasons to follow beneficial practices such as good culture, inspection and close observation, and adhering to a strict policy of quarantining (isolating) new plants.

INSPECTION

Use the following trouble-shooting methods for *all* newly acquired plants. Even the most careful growers and nurseries occasionally have pest problems.

Upper-side inspection: Look for aphids, thrips, cyclamen mite damage, and foliar mealybugs.

Bottom-side inspection: Turn the root ball out of the pot and carefully search for soil mealybugs or unhealthy roots.

If any of these pests are found during inspection, follow the procedures recommended for the specific pest.

Leaf cuttings: Wash leaves in mild detergent suds and rinse well.

ISOLATION

If you do not see soil or foliar mealybugs or any other pests, *isolating or quarantining newly acquired plants is still mandatory.* For most pests, only the adults are visible to the naked eye and other life stages may be present but unknown to you. Investing in a 20x magnifying loupe is well worth the cost.

Steps may be taken to keep pests and pathogens from getting into the plant room in the first place. All newly acquired plants should be disbudded before brought into the house. The most logical and most frequently recommended advice is to isolate all new plants for thirty to forty-five days before placing them into your collection. This is good advice, but in practical application it doesn't work.

Few growers reserve a well-lighted, well-located area for the exclusive use of new plant isolation; most growers already have plants in that kind of space. Even if such an area could be set aside, what happens when more new plants are brought in and the ones in isolation haven't cleared the recommended period?

It is possible to isolate a few plants by placing them in clear plastic bags and delegating one shelf of a light stand for these plants. The extra humidity would benefit plants that have just been repotted and give the plants time to acclimate to the new environment while protecting the rest of the collection from possible infestation.

NON-CHEMICAL PREVENTION

Insecticidal soaps and botanical oils may be used to treat all incoming plants and leaves. *Disbudding, repotting, and isolating must accompany these non-chemical treatments.*

PREVENTIVE CHEMICAL TREATMENT

If it is not possible to isolate all incoming plants, many growers choose to treat all incoming plants with a combination of chemicals to prevent mealybugs, thrips and mites from infesting their collection even if no pests are observed during inspection. *IMPORTANT: Any chemical treatment for thrips and mites must be repeated three times at seven- to ten-day intervals.* (See Thrips, p. 106, and Cyclamen Mites, p. 104, for life-cycle information and Pesticide Arsenal, p. 111, for information on specific pesticides.)

If you can't isolate, it is better to treat all incoming plants than to risk infesting the rest of your collection. Following all of these procedures makes it reasonably safe to put newly acquired plants into your collection, but keep a sharp eye on them for the next thirty days or so.

FOLLOW-UP PRECAUTIONS

If inspection, isolation, and follow-up precautions are followed faithfully, you may never need to consult the rest of this chapter.

1. Keep the windows in the plant room closed. Aphids and thrips can come in through the screens. Introduce fresh air indirectly from a nearby room.

2. Do not enter the plant room after working in the garden without washing hands and changing clothes.

3. To be on the safe side, avoid keeping other types of plants (except possibly others in the gesneriad family) with African violets. For example the ivy family often comes with built-in red spider mites.

4. Cut flowers, too, can bring their own mites and thrips. Do not place them in the same room with African violets.

5. Don't put new plants on common watering sources such as capillary matting or wicks in a common reservoir; use an individual saucer for each pot. The one exception could be trays of miniatures or plantlets for convenience in watering.

6. Pot on layers of newspaper. Remove the top layer of paper before working with the next plant. This may avoid passing along undiscovered mealybugs, thrips, or mites to the next plant. Dip tools frequently in a 10% bleach solution

Pests

Insect and mite pests damage plants by chewing or sucking. Chewing pests leave holes or other evidence; they are usually visible and can be picked off or washed off with a spray of warm water. Sucking pests feed by inserting their mouthparts into the plant tissue and sucking the plant's juices. Aphids, mealybugs, thrips and mites are all sucking pests.

APHIDS

What to look for: Readily visible insects that come in a variety of colors and congregate on foliage, peduncles, and blossoms.

How to get rid of them: Use a broad-spectrum pesticide spray. Check the label to be sure it is recommended for African violets. Follow the directions and heed all warnings. Check again the next day or so to be sure there are no survivors. Test the spray to be sure it does not discolor foliage or blossoms; spray at the recommended distance. Avid® insecticide/miticide is effective in eliminating aphids and it does not discolor the foliage.

BROAD MITE & RED SPIDER MITE

What to look for: Distorted or bleached leaves. Broad mites feed on the undersides of mature leaves causing the leaf edges to curl down. Red spider mites cause the foliage to have a bleached appearance; a fine webbing will be evident.

How to get rid of them: The treatment for both is the same as for cyclamen mites. They are not as common on African violets as are cyclamen mites. Some of the newer miticides are mite specific; know which mites are present.

CYCLAMEN MITES

Even with a microscope, cyclamen mites are hard to see. As soon as the scope light hits them, they hide under leaves and petioles. The hobbyist grower chiefly needs to learn how to recognize the damage typical of mites so they can be stopped before the damage becomes widespread or severe. If you have not experienced a mite infestation, don't miss a chance to observe mite-infested plants of growers who haven't been as fortunate. A first-hand view enables you to recognize the signs early on.

What to look for: Centers that seem to be unusually tight and/or a slight graying at the base of the new center leaves. Mites suck the juice of the tender leaves so the graying is a result of the leaf hairs' becoming more prominent following the shrinkage of the tissue. These leaves are very brittle, hard, and stunted. The new buds are also twisted and stunted.

How to get rid of them: Once mite damage is found on one plant, it must be assumed that the entire collection is infested. Mites can be spread by fingers or tools as well as from leaves touching. Spray every plant and don't forget leaf cuttings and plantlets. After you become a mite expert, you may opt to spray just the shelf-mates of the affected plant, but be alert. If plants on other shelves show signs of damage, spray the rest of the collection.

1. Mix a miticide (Kelthane®, Avid or another miticide) according to directions. Add a few drops of a spreader-activator* with water slightly warmer than tepid (about 80°F). The water will cool as it passes through the air, but using hot water can change the reaction of the chemicals.

*Spreader-activator is a wetting agent that mixes with water to reduce the surface tension that causes water to bead. The solution then penetrates to the base of the hairs of petioles and leaves where some of the mites may otherwise survive safe and dry. A commercial spreader-activator is preferred over dish detergent as a wetting agent. No matter how much the foliage is soaked during spraying, the solution won't spot the leaves or leave a residue. Check labels for proper quantities.

2. Spray thoroughly, particularly the center of the crown where the youngest leaves are. Mites prefer the young center leaves. Pick the plant up and spray into and under the foliage, covering the underside of the leaves and petioles.

3. Spray two more times at five- to seven-day intervals. A life cycle may be completed in from one to three weeks; repeat spraying is necessary to eliminate the newly hatched larvae and recently emerged adult stage mites. Mix a fresh batch of solution each time. The only way mites can be killed with leftover solution is by drowning!

It is nearly always unwise to try to save a show plant that has severe cyclamen mite damage. Instead, take a leaf for propagation and wash it thoroughly in the miticide solution.

If it is a prime show specimen and you seriously want to save that plant, isolate it, spray the plant, and allow suckers to form. Pick off all but one and root it when it is big enough, following the directions for propagating suckers. Discard the rest of the plant.

FUNGUS GNATS

What to look for: No problem here; if there is the slightest movement around the plants, gnats fly out of the pots. They are more irritating than harmful, but they must be dealt with for your peace of mind if nothing else.

How to get rid of *them:* Hang a no-pest strip on each light stand for a few weeks; follow the recommended precautions, and be sure the strip is safe for use in the home. Spray the soil surface of each pot lightly with a pesticide spray. Do this every day for ten days or so and the population will be greatly reduced if not eliminated entirely.

FOLIAR MEALYBUG

About the time you think you have gotten rid of them for good, these pests crop up again. Unless a plant is an irreplaceable variety, the whole thing should be put into a plastic bag (tape it

shut) and taken to the trashcan. But if you are determined to keep the plant or plants, don't be casual about the treatment. Bring out the big guns and don't rest until the critters are gone.

What to look for: White cottony specks on petioles, in axils, and on backs of leaves.

How to get rid of *them:* Isolate the infested plant or plants by putting them in a plastic bag. If only a few plants are involved, dip a cotton swab in alcohol and touch each cottony speck with it. Search every day and repeat as necessary.

If the infestation is advanced, spray the entire collection, after swabbing, with an insecticide such as Malathion or Avid. Repeat three more times at seven-day intervals. Use all recommended precautions. Marathon®1% granular systemic added to the soil is a preventive against foliar mealybugs.

SOIL MEALYBUG

Soil mealybugs are sucking pests that feed on plant roots. Adults resemble small insets that have been rolled in white four. Adults and their cottony egg masses are usually on the outside of the root ball, and can be seen when the plant is lifted from the container. Damage symptoms are non-specific and usually involve slow growth and generally unhealthy looking plants. The outside leaves wilt as though they aren't getting enough water.

Females (there are no males) lay eggs in the cottony masses, which hatch into tiny crawlers. At this stage, they may be dispersed among plants, often in the irrigation water. The life cycle from egg to adult is from 2 to 4 months and the adults can live nearly 60 days, producing three batches of eggs. Mealybugs are most likely introduced into a collection from purchasing infested plants and are most commonly spread when an infested pot is passed over other plants; the insects drop out of the bottom of the pot on whatever is below.

What to look for: Very small, white, oval waxy specks that resemble pieces of perlite. Prod one with a pin; if it is a mealybug, it will move, but ever so slowly. If the infestation is heavy, they also cluster above the soil line around the base of the main stem and into the lower axils of the petioles.

How to get rid of *them:* It may be advisable to throw out plants with a bad infestation. If you can't stand that, take the crowns and repot them in clean pots with new soil, put Marathon in the soil, and isolate the plants in plastic bags for several weeks

Prevention: Repot all plants when you bring them home applying granular Marathon systemic to the soil as a preventive. Isolate plants on separate reservoirs for a month. (See Pesticides section for more on Marathon use.)

NEMATODES

Nematodes were a problem when growers mixed their own soil using garden loam. They are rarely a problem when the grower uses soil-less potting mix.

What to *look for:* There are both soil and foliar nematodes. As with cyclamen mites, these pests can only be seen through dissection of roots and petioles under a microscope.

How to *get rid of them:* The chemical drench required is dangerous to use and the plant would never be the same again, anyway. As with soil mealybugs, a trip to the trash can is the best way to get rid of them. Since nematodes sometime penetrate into the petioles, *there is some risk in taking a leaf for propagation.* If the variety is a valuable one, it is reasonably safe to take the crown with just the three small center leaves and repot it, and isolate it.

SPRINGTAILS

What to *look for:* Small, light-colored pests that scurry around on the bottom of pots and in saucers. They are capable of jumping a distance many times their body length. They feed on decaying organic material and thrive under moist, warm conditions.

How to *get rid of them:* Ignore them. They do very little damage to the overall health of the plant. Don't drench with chemicals and especially not with a chlorine bleach solution as is sometimes advised. You know what even a very dilute solution does to your hands. Imagine what it does to the delicate feeder roots of an African violet.

THRIPS

The word is thrips–please don't drop the "s." One thrips is a thrips and a dozen thrips are thrips! Thrips feed by rasping and sucking plant fluids, which distort and discolor the blossoms. Feeding on the pollen causes the blossoms to wilt prematurely.

Thrips develop from egg to adult in 10-15 days in hot, dry conditions; up to 57 days at cooler temperatures. They go through five developmental stages: egg, larva (two instars), two transformation stages, and adult.

What to look for: Thrips can be seen with the naked eye. They lay eggs in the anthers and sometimes even in slits they make in the leaves. Flick the anthers with your fingernail or lightly blow on the blossom and watch closely. Be patient. Sometimes it may take a few seconds for them to scurry into sight. Ugh! The sight strikes dread in the heart of any grower, especially at show time. If you see one, assume a multitude!

Look for yellow pollen spilled on blossoms, small bruise-like spots at the juncture of the petal lobes, white streaks on the blossoms, and, with a heavy infestation, fine, silvery streaks on the backs of the leaves.

How to *get rid of them:* Thrips are very hard to get rid of and since they can fly, they travel rapidly from plant to plant. So don't take a chance; treat the entire collection. Do it right the first time or you will be going through the process again, and again, and again!

1. Remove all blossoms and buds including the smallest forming buds and the entire blossom stem.

2. Several products may be used for thrips: Malathion, Orthene®, Conserve SC®, Avid, and Pylon®. All are concentrated and are mixed, according to label instructions, with warm water. Spray both sides of the foliage thoroughly. See p. 111 for more information on these insecticides.

3. Repeat two more times at seven- to ten-day intervals *following all recommended precautions.* Because of the thrips reproductive stages, the repeat applications of insecticide are necessary.

4. If thrips reappear within a few weeks, use a different insecticide and repeat the treatment.

Thrips follow-up: As each plant comes back into bloom, inspect carefully for thrips. Close scrutiny is essential. If one thrips on one plant is missed, you will have to go through the process all over again. Yes, *one!* It was discouraging to learn that it doesn't take even a breeding pair to perpetuate the species. (Now you know why they are so tough to get rid of.) Be especially diligent just before completely disbudding before a show. Treatment can be started at that time but not once the blossoms have opened. Most insecticides discolor blossoms; however, Conserve SC does not damage the blossoms and may be used at show time. Marathon systemic is labeled for thrips, but its molecular structure doesn't allow it to move into the blossoms of the African Violet.

From entomologist Dr. Charles Cole, Texas Agricultural Extension Service: *Several species of thrips occur on African violets. Some are easily controlled with Malathion. Unfortunately the most common species* on *violets is the western flower thrips,* <u>*Frankliniella occidentalis,*</u> *and is difficult* to *control. Malathion will not touch this species; however, Orthene is fairly effective. Where* a *heavy infestation occurs, disbudding enhances control. Also, two to three applications at seven-day intervals are usually needed* to *get control.*

Use Orthene soluble-powder rather than liquid Orthene. The liquid has a *petroleum additive that may* be *concentrated enough to damage foliage.*

Dr Cole also mentioned that when the plant blooms again the blossoms may be an off-color. This is not a permanent sporting and the blossoms should return to normal color in subsequent bloom cycles.

Pathogens

A pathogen is an organism or virus capable of causing diseases in a host plant. The best defense against plant disease is proper cultural procedures, good environmental conditions, and the application of basic sanitary practices. The world of plant disease (pathogen) management has benefited from new products that when used as preventatives inhibit the pathogen from invading the plant (See Fungicides, p. 112).

FUNGUS

Root rot, crown rot, leaf rot, damping-off, gray mold, and related diseases (see separate listings for powdery mildew and botrytis) are all types of fungus.

What to look for: Some types of fungus damage resemble cyclamen mite damage. For instance, PYTHIUM FUNGUS affects roots and root damage that results in a gray, stunted appearance of the crown, and finally the collapse of the entire plant. At first, CROWN ROT resembles cyclamen mite damage. As these fungi progress, the center leaves will be soft instead of turgid; eventually the crown turns brown and rots away. The first signs of LEAF ROT are seen on the outer leaves and petioles, which become light gray and finally a translucent brown with a jelly-like consistency. DAMPING-OFF causes small seedlings to suddenly wilt and collapse.

Prevention: The best approach is to alter adverse environmental conditions and improper cultural procedures. Healthy, vigorous plants grown under controlled conditions resist fungus attacks. Provide a growing area where moderate temperature range and good ventilation can be maintained. You may have to invest in a fan, air conditioner, or dehumidifier.

Fungi thrive when the soil has poor aeration, is of a greater depth than the roots can utilize, and is kept too wet. Aeration in the perlite layer and in the porous potting mix, thus controlling soil moisture, creates resistance to fungi.

It may seem contradictory, but allowing plants to become too dry can also set them up for fungus attack (most commonly crown rot). Many of the fine feeder roots die. When proper watering is resumed, the uptake of water is severely restricted and over-wetness of the soil results.

Keep the growing area clean and free of dead blossoms, soil particles, and mold. Remove spent blossoms. When repotting, dip tools in dilute bleach solution before working on the next plant. Scrub used pots thoroughly in detergent.

If there are fungus problems in your area, take additional precautions. Wipe down all trays and work areas; soak pots in a dilute bleach solution. Use about twenty parts water to one part bleach (approximately 3/4 cup bleach to one gallon of water). Mix up a fresh solution each time since the chlorine content of the solution dissipates in about four hours.

BOTRYTIS

What to look for: Botrytis is a fungus disease, which may appear as a gray fuzzy mold on the surface of blossoms or buds. The blossoms become mushy and tan or gray; they look like the color has been sucked out. Botrytis also appears inside the plant structure and leaves loose their stiffness. This is a common cause of failure of leaf cuttings.

High humidity, cool temperature and lack of air movement create the environment for botrytis to develop. It can be spread by cutting utensils, hands, insects, and the grower's failure to remove leaves and moldy blossoms immediately.

Prevention and control: Keep the humidity at or below 60%; avoid over-watering; maintain air circulation; and keep the plant area clean. Spray affected plants with a fungicide.

POWDERY MILDEW

Powdery mildew is also a fungus, but most growers, no matter what their growing conditions, will experience an occasional problem with it. There is such a thing as "mildew weather," usually in the early spring when humidity rises and the days begin to warm up, but the nights are still cold.

What to look for: A whitish-gray, frosty sprinkling on the foliage. It is sometimes found on just one side of the plant where the foliage is against a wall or other dead-air space. Blossoms and peduncles may also be involved. Do NOT ignore it! It can ruin a plant if allowed to go unchecked.

How to get rid of it: Run a small fan during light hours to circulate the air, keep humidity to about 50% to 60%, and try to keep the daytime and nighttime temperature variance to no more than ten degrees.

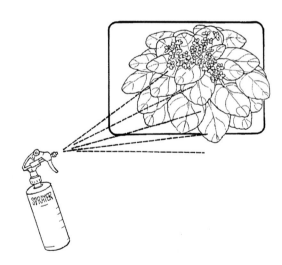

Several home remedies include adding a pinch of baking soda to water in a spray bottle to treat the mildew. Another common product used to control mildew is powdered sulfur. Mix 1/2 teaspoon sulfur to one cup warm water and shake vigorously; spray the entire plant. This will not harm the blossoms.

Lysol disinfectant spray works for occasional spots of mildew. Spray it directly on the mildew. It won't mar foliage, but it (especially the aerosol spray) will discolor blossoms and damage crowns. If the aerosol is used, spray above the plants and let the mist settle. During mildew weather, spray Lysol along walls, windowsills, floors, and on tray matting. Use 1/4-teaspoon Lysol concentrate to one pint of warm water in a sprayer. Repeat at weekly intervals or as needed, and take all recommended precautions.

A number of fungicides are available at garden centers. If you use one, test it on one or two plants before using it on your whole collection. (See fungicides in the Pesticide Arsenal section, p. 112.)

VIRUS

Violet virus are rare. The symptoms imitate other problems and are difficult to diagnose. There is no cure, and affected plants must be discarded. If a viral disease is suspected, consult county or state agricultural services for an opinion. Good sanitary procedures and eradicating pests (virus carriers) will lessen the possibility of a virus problem.

Physiological Problems

LEAF SPOTTING

Water spots and ring spots are the most common, but other patterns of leaf discoloration may occur.

What to *look for:* True to its name, ring-spot is a matter of light-colored (often yellowish) ring-shaped spots, or sometimes irregular splotches and track-like marks. All of these are caused by any insult to the plant such as cold drafts or cold water on the roots or foliage, allowing the soil to go dry, potting down a long neck, burns from direct sun-rays, and so on. Sometimes spotting occurs merely because the variety is very sensitive to changes.

Water spots are dull spots on foliage caused by etching from salts in fertilizer solution or mineral content of water.

How to *prevent it:* Introduce fresh air from another room to avoid drafts and use room temperature water. To avoid water spotting, pat up drops spilled on foliage with a tissue or sponge and pat up excess water after washing plants. Use tepid water to wash plants. Room temperature water can be used for spraying plants during hot, dry wind conditions and will not spot foliage if a fine mist sprayer is used. Use rainwater, distilled water, reverse osmosis, or softened water for mixing sprays to avoid mineral deposits on the foliage. A small amount of softened water used to spray the leaves will not harm the plant.

LEAF TIP BURN

Tip burn occurs on mature plants and the damage is permanent. Tempting as it may be to reach out and remove a brown leaf tip with your thumbnail, remember that leaf trimming is not permitted in a judged show.

What to *look for:* Brown spots on the tips of the leaves and sometimes along the edges. This condition is usually found only on the outer row of leaves and is caused by fertilizer salts build-up.

How to *prevent it:* Repotting every four months and following all recommended procedures usually keep the problem to a minimum. Some varieties are more susceptible than others. If you have a favorite show plant that often tip burns, leach the soil with plain water about once a month. Otherwise, don't give shelf space to those varieties that are particularly susceptible to tip burn.

ORANGE CRUST

What to *look for:* A rusty-orange, crystal-like substance on the hairs of the center leaves. This is a build-up of fertilizer salts that affects young plants, and is caused by a combination of an immature root system, a too-heavy or too-rich soil mix, over-watering, and over-fertilizing. *How* to *prevent it*: Follow the directions for potting up and watering plantlets.

How to *save affected plants:* The foliage will be permanently damaged if action isn't taken. Pour warm water over the plant to dissolve the salt crystals and to leach the soil mix. Take care not to over-water for the next week or so. However, don't stop fertilizing because soilless potting mixes are usually deficient in nutrients and newly potted plants need a constant supply of nutrients, particularly nitrogen.

To extend the intervals between watering, commercial nurseries often use a heavier soil mix than the hobbyist grower does. When we buy nursery-grown African violets and subject them to our watering schedule, they sometimes develop an orange crust. If this occurs, and if the plantlet looks sturdy with a five- or six-inch leaf span, wash the crystals off with warm water and pot into a 4" tub pot. It often pays to repot newly acquired plants immediately.

WHITE RESIDUE

What to look for: White spots on the edges of the leaves are dried condensation; it occurs during "mildew weather"–a series of warm days, cold nights, and high humidity. Check the plants early in the morning and drops of dew may be seen along the leaf edges. (This is called "guttation.") Dark foliage seems to form condensation more readily than light-colored foliage. Drops of water allowed to dry on foliage may also leave a ring of white residue if the water is alkaline.

How to *get rid of it*: A spit-dampened thumb seems to work about as well as anything else. If that doesn't appeal to you, try sponging the spots with a solution of a few drops of vinegar to one cup of water. If you have the time and patience, wipe the dew from the edges of the leaves each morning before it gets a chance to dry.

YELLOW LEAF EDGE

What to look for: A yellow or cream-colored band around the edges of the leaves (sometimes called "haloing"). The cause is hard to determine. Some varieties have a tendency to develop a yellow edge; it may be boron defiance or transplant shock. Nitrogen deficiency causes the outer leaves to turn yellow at the tips and then the yellowing moves evenly up the leaf.

How to prevent it: Check the pH of the soil mix. If the pH is too acid or too alkaline, some of the nutrients will not be assimilated properly. Use water with a low salt content. Pot down a long neck before it gets too long; this lessens the chance of transplant shock. A nitrogen deficiency sometimes occurs on show plants that have been on a long schedule of very low nitrogen bloom booster fertilizer before a show. A few applications of 20-20-20 fertilizer usually corrects the problem.

LEAF BLEACHING

The leaves of African violets grown under fluorescent lights bleach out slightly about two hours before the end of the light period. The part of the leaves exposed to light becomes a lighter green with a pinkish-red cast. When a leaf that overlaps another is lifted, the covered part of the leaf is the usual shade. Varieties with very dark leaves show little or no bleaching. If the leaves start to bleach earlier than two hours before the lights go off, it may mean that the plants are not getting enough fertilizer. If they don't bleach at all, it may mean that the plants are being over-fertilized. However, this method of determining proper feeding is not accurate. Appreciate this interesting phenomenon but continue using the recommended amounts of fertilizer.

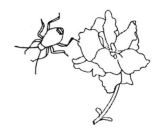

Many new laws have been enacted in the past decade that have greatly changed the status of pesticide availability and registered uses. New criteria for considering residues and potential effects on humans have been responsible for many well-known compounds disappearing from standard use in recent years.

Various state and federal laws control the availability and use of pesticides and insecticides; some of the following products may not be available in every state.

Check labels to be sure that the pesticide is approved by the EPA for your specific need. The label of every product should be read before purchase and use, and remember–*the label is the law*.

Most labels recommend that a mixed product be used the day it is mixed. Keep all concentrated insecticides and pesticides tightly closed and out of reach of children and away from food products. *Follow all safety precautions.*

Extend the shelf life of pesticides and fungicides by keeping them tightly capped and storing them in a cool, dark place. Check the labels for possible expiration dates.

The Material Safety Data Sheet (MSDS) includes a great deal of information on pesticides, including first aid, toxicological, and ecological information. The MSDS for any pesticide is available on the Internet; type the trade or chemical name of the product, followed by MSDS in an internet search engine.

Follow safety precautions when using any chemical products. Common sense practices such as avoiding inhalation and skin contact with chemicals should be followed. Wear disposable plastic gloves and long sleeves. Don't handle the plants until they are dry. Read the safety precautions for every product.

Research in chemical pesticides is being conducted on many products that have commercial value and may eventually be labeled as safe for in home use for African violets. New chemical families of insecticides are being developed that work on very specific nerve areas of insects and have low toxicity for humans. Some newer products have *translaminar* capabilities, meaning that when applied as a foliar spray, the compound moves into the foliage. They do not become systemic, but come into contact with hard to reach pests that systemic products don't usually reach. Miticides are becoming mite specific; some work for broad mites, some for cyclamen mites, etc. Again, check the label.

There are many things to watch for in the coming years that may make the control of pests and pathogens simple and safe.

The following products are currently used by violet growers and have low human toxicity. They may be used indoors if labeled precautions are followed.

The mention of these brand name products does not constitute an endorsement of the product by AVSA.

AVID® 0.15EC, a miticide/insecticide, is effective in the control of mites and other sucking and chewing insects including thrips. The active ingredient is *abamectin.*

How to use: Mix according to label instructions with warm water in a spray bottle and thoroughly spray the entire plant. Avid is effective against adult and immature mites working both on contact and through ingestion. It is translaminar and will penetrate the leaf surface of young, tender foliage to provide two to three weeks of residual control. *Pylon®* is labeled for control of broad and cyclamen mites and thrips on African violets. The active ingredient is *chlorfenapyr*, the first in a new pyrole chemical class. It has some translaminar activity.

Forbid® 4F and Judo® are in a new miticide /insecticide class with the common name *spiromesifen.* By preventing lipid synthesis in the insect's body, it becomes lethal. It is labeled for control of whiteflies and mites from egg through adult stages.

Conserve SC® (suspension concentrate) is used to control thrips. The common name for Conserve is *spinosad.* Mix with water according to instructions. Spray the entire plant, including blooms, three times at seven- to ten-day intervals with uniform coverage of both upper and lower leaf surface. Conserve will not damage blooms. Do not reapply within less than 7 days and rotate control.

Marathon ® 1% granular systemic insecticide is used to control aphids, mealybugs, thrips, and whiteflies. The active ingredient in Marathon is *imidacloprid.* Marathon is effective in the control of soil mealybugs, but it is less effective in controlling thrips in African violets due to its molecular structure; it does not get absorbed into the blossoms. Imidacloprid is not a contact insecticide. The chemical works only after the plant absorbs the chemical and the insect eats into the plant.

When repotting, sprinkle Marathon on the potting mix before inserting the plant in the pot; do not dump it in one spot. The amount of Marathon depends on the size of pot; follow directions. Marathon may be sprinkled around the top of the potting mix in the pot and watered in. Do not over-water as Marathon may be washed out; do not apply if the potting mix is water logged or saturated. Apply once every sixteen weeks.

Neem oil, a biopesticide sold under a number of different brand names, is labeled as a fungicide/insecticide/miticide product derived from neem seed oil. This botanical oil may be used indoors safely. As a fungicide, neem oil is a preventative as well as a curative. It acts to coat fungal spores and then dehydrates them to stop the cycle. As a miticide or insecticide it acts as a suffocant and is should not be used for these purposes.

Insecticidal soaps, sold under a number of different brand names, are marginally effective against pests on African violets. They are broadly labeled. Soap may be used as a mite population knock-down, so that a conventional product can be used more effectively against a smaller population.

Fungicides: A number of new fungicides are registered for nurseries and greenhouse use for control of botrytis and other fungal diseases. Decree®, Dithane®, and Medallion® are registered for use on African violets.

Less expensive fungicides used by African violet growers are available at garden centers; they may not be labeled for African violets but have been reported as safe and effective. These include Green Light Fungaway® and Ortho Rose Pride®.

Always test a new product on one or two plants, even if it is registered for use on African violets

Physan 20® is a general bactericide, fungicide, virucide and algaecide. It controls algae on mats, wicks, reservoirs, trays, pots, benches and work surfaces; controls damping off on seedlings and plants; controls crown rot, powdery mildew, botrytis; controls disease spread by disinfecting tools (from package insert).

Physan 20 may be added to the plant water, which helps to control algae formation in wicking trays and on matting. To inhibit transfer of disease use one tablespoon per gallon of water for sanitizing tools, pots and trays. Foliage may be sprayed for control of mildew, however, complete coverage of all plant surfaces is important; follow instructions for amount to use.

Phyton 27® is a bactericide and fungicide for control of powdery mildew and botrytis. Use according to directions. Spray every ten to fourteen days to prevent disease. Spray to wet when disease appears and repeat every five to seven days as needed for powdery mildew. Read the instructions before using.

UPDATE ON OLDER PRODUCTS

Malathion, an organophosphate insecticide of relatively low toxicity to humans, has been used for a number of years for thrips. It is available in garden supply centers.

Orthene 75 S soluble powder (*acephate*) is used to control chewing and sucking insects such as aphids, thrips, and whiteflies. It is also listed as a miticide. *Use with caution and follow all safety precautions.* Mix according to directions. Mix outdoors. Its strong odor is not offensive once the powder is diluted.

Kelthane (*dicofol*) is a miticide available in garden supply centers. It has been used as a drench or a spray. Mix according to directions with warm water and thoroughly spray plants.

WHY PRODUCTS FAIL

Information from a university extension bulletin gave several reasons why disease and pest management in horticulture industries fail. The points are applicable to African violet growers:

- Not implementing continued observations. Regular monitoring the plants in your collection is the backbone of your pest management.

- Improper diagnosis; know the exact problem being treated. Incorrect diagnosis generally leads to improper treatments, which often results in greater problems.

- The use of the incorrect pesticide for the problem or not following through with the treatment. For example, you cannot spray for thrips or mites just one time.

- Over-reliance on pesticide products; only treating when necessary is the real long-term solution.

HOW TO STAY CURRENT WITH NEW PRODUCTS

The influx of new insecticide, miticide, and fungicide products is almost over-whelming, even for the professional extension entomologists but they have the most current information available. University cooperative extensive services have information bulletins on pests and pesticides on their websites. Companies have information bulletins on the products they manufacture and sell.

Basically this section dealt with commercial chemical products. There are also a number of non-chemical alternatives. Sticky strips for flying insects and insecticidal soaps for spraying and drenching are good non-chemical products. Refer to an organic gardening book for more information on non-chemical alternatives.

And don't forget local AVSA affiliates and horticulture clubs. This is one of the best places to learn what products and practices the growers in your area are using.

REFERENCES:

YOU CAN Grow African Violets by Kent and Joyce Stork, AVSA, 2007. See the chapter on "What You Need to Know about Pests and Pesticides."

Insect and Mite Pests of African Violets by Dr. Charles Cole, revised 2003

The AVSA Handbook for Growers, Exhibitors, and Judges contains a section on the general prevention and control of pests and diseases.

Contact your local or state Cooperative Extension Office for information on pesticides that are currently registered for home use in your area.

Search the Internet for University Extension Bulletins, Material Safety Data Sheets (MSDS) and product manufacturer's websites.

Saintpaulia History

In 1892, while serving as district governor of Tanganyika, East Africa (now Tanzania), Baron Walter von Saint Paul discovered an unusual flowering plant in the nearby Usambara Mountains. He sent seeds, and possibly plants, to his father, Baron Ulrich von Saint Paul, in Germany. Saint Paul shared them with Hermann Wendland, director of the Royal Botanic Gardens of Germany, who concluded that the plant was an entirely new species.

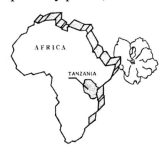

He named it *Saintpaulia ionantlia. Saintpaulia,* in honor of the father and son who were responsible for bringing it to the attention of botanists and *ionantha,* which is Greek for "with violet-like flowers." Many years later a sharp-eyed botanist discovered that Baron von Saint Paul had actually sent two species from Africa. The second species was appropriately named *Saintpaulia confusa.*

Saintpaulias arrived in the United States in 1893. W. K. Harris, a Philadelphia florist, obtained plants from a New York dealer who had received a shipment from Europe. "The violet from Africa" became popularly known as African violet. Actually, true violets belong to the Violaceae family; *Saintpaulias* belong to the Gesneriaceae family.

In 1927 Armacost and Royston Nursery in Los Angeles, California, ordered *Saintpaulia* seeds from Germany and England. From the resulting seedlings, ten were selected as having the most desirable characteristics to use for breeding stock. Two–'Blue Boy' and 'Sailor Boy'– were from the German seedlings. Those chosen from among the English seedlings were 'Admiral,' 'Amethyst,' 'Commodore,' 'Mermaid,' 'Neptune,' 'Norseman,' 'Number 32,' and 'Viking.' All

were single blossoms in hues of violet, blue, and purple. The majority of the beautiful and diverse varieties we enjoy today come from the original two species and the ten Armacost and Royston seedlings.

Dr. B.L. Burtt studied the genus *Saintpaulia* in the 1940's-1960's and published a taxonomy system that recognized 20 species and four varieties. He based much of his work on seed and leaf material sent to him by collectors in Africa and grown at the Royal Botanic Gardens, Edinburgh and Kew. The plants from the original wild collections could be reasonably identifiable from each other and the division of the genus into species developed by Dr. Burtt has persisted until just recently. When the African Violet Society of America established registration or identification numbers for the *Saintpaulia* species, the taxonomy system of Dr. Burtt was the one used.

In the last 20 years, additional plants from the wild have become available and spread among growers. Most notable are plants from the Mather collection and the Uppsala Botanical Garden. Because of the discovery of these new plants, questions have been raised as to how to classify them. Based on DNA evidence from several studies and more extensive field collections of plants, Dr. Iain Darbyshire, Royal Botanical Gardens, Kew, England, has recently proposed a new taxonomic classification of the species in genus Saintpaulia. His system was published in 2006 in the "Flora of Tropical East Africa, Gesneriaceae." This system acknowledges the high degree of similarity between the species and reduces the number from 20 to 6. In recognition of Burtt's classification system, several of the plants have been reclassified into subspecies using their former species name.

The African Violet Society of America registration numbers for the species will soon be updated to reflect the newer classification system.

African Violet Society of America, Inc.

The African Violet Society of America, Inc. (founded in 1946) maintains a national office in Beaumont, Texas. The society is usually referred to by initials instead of the full name; when using the initials, pronounce each letter separately–AVSA.

The stated purposes of the association are to stimulate interest in the propagation and culture of the African violet; promote distribution of cultivars and species; and publish reliable, practical information of interest to members. AVSA is a clearinghouse of information about African violets.

AVSA holds a national convention each spring. In addition, local and regional affiliates hold annual shows and sales. For information about affiliates or affiliate shows near you, go to the AVSA website. AVSA has a large international membership with affiliates in many countries.

Membership is open to anyone interested in African violets. To join AVSA , write, call, or go to the website for current dues to:

African Violet Society of America, Inc.
2375 North Street
Beaumont, Texas 77702
Phone: 409-839-4725

Website: www.avsa.org

AVSA PUBLICATIONS:

AVSA issues several publications listed below. Request a current price list from the AVSA office or from the website.

AFRICAN VIOLET MAGAZINE: The *AVM* is included as a part of AVSA membership and is published six times a year with full color pictures and informative articles.

AFRICAN VIOLET MASTER LIST OF SPECIES AND CULTIVARS (AVML): Lists all registered and most non-registered varieties. AVSA is the International Registration Authority for the genus *Saintpaulia* (African violet) and was designated as such by the Council of the International Society for Horticulture and Science. This publication is also commonly referred to as the Master Variety List (MVL)

The *AVML* lists the varieties, descriptions, registration numbers, and the hybridizer (plus all recognized species) from the beginning of registration on February 25, 1949. The *AVML* is updated six times a year. Check the "Registration Report" column in the *AVM* for updated information. Keep it up-to-date by noting corrections and new varieties listed in the magazine; file this information with the current *AVML*.

FIRST CLASS (FC): A software interactive database that contains names, descriptions, hybridizers, and registration information for over 15,318 African violet cultivars and species (as of September 2007), as well as over 5,704 photos of 3,904 cultivars. More cultivars and photos are added regularly to the database, with an average of approximately 25 to 50 new cultivars and 100 to 150 new photos every two months.

The database may be searched by plant name; hybridizer; photos; size, type, color of blossom, and more. The user may add notes for any listed variety as well as adding a "user database" of varieties not in the *FC* database. Personal photos may be added to the database. This database, which is updated six times a year, may be purchased from the AVSA office.

GROWING TO SHOW, written and illustrated by Pauline Bartholomew in 1985. Rights to this book were given to AVSA in 2003. Revised by AVSA in 2008.

INSECT AND MITE PESTS OF AFRICAN VIOLETS by Charles L. Cole (Revised, 2003). This publication was written as a reference for helping African violet growers become more proficient in detecting, identifying and controlling pests.

THE AVSA HANDBOOK FOR AFRICAN VIOLET GROWERS, EXHIBITORS, AND JUDGES: The *Handbook* contains the rules and regulations for African violet shows, judges, judging, plus other valuable information for exhibitors. This Handbook is a "must" for all exhibitors and judges. Growers will find useful information on all aspects of growing African violets. Keep the *Handbook* up-to-date by noting any additions or changes published in the *AVM* "Shows & Judges" column.

YOU CAN GROW AFRICAN VIOLETS, The Official Guide Authorized by the African Violet Society of America, (2007) by Kent and Joyce Stork. The book is designed for beginners with little experience but is also useful for advanced growers who similarly struggle to keep all aspects of growing in balance. It may be purchased through iUniverse Publishing or the AVSA website.

WEBSITE: The AVSA website, includes: membership information; contact information for AVSA affiliates by state and region; list of commercial sellers of African violet plants and supplies with contact information, including web sites and e-mail addresses; a photo gallery with several hundred photos of African violets; *FAQ* – Frequently Asked Questions; *AVM Index* – a searchable index of articles from the *African Violet Magazine* from 1947 (Vol. 1) to current year; the AVSA Store where all of the above publications can be purchased; and much more.

Glossary

The following are definitions of the terms used in this manual and terms with which the African violet grower and exhibitor should be familiar.

ANTHERS: The expanded tip of the stamen consisting of one or more pairs of lobes which contain the pollen.

AXIL: The angle formed at the juncture of the petiole and the main stem.

BLOOM STALK: The peduncle, pedicels, and blossoms as a unit.

BLOSSOM COLORS: Blossom color is one means by which African violets are classified for competitive showing. The *AVML* and *First Class* give the official color description of the varieties. This description is usually furnished by the hybridizer.

BLOSSOM TYPES: Blossoms are described in the *AVML* as single, double, or semidouble. The blossom type is another means of classifying African violets for competitive showing. The *AVML* also lists bell-shaped, fringed, ruffled, and wasp as blossom types.

CHIMERA: A plant composed of two or more genetically different tissues growing separately but adjacent to each other in one plant; these tissues are commonly arranged in layers. (See Learn the Language – Blossom Types.) Note: Foliage can also be chimera.

COLLECTION: Any number of plants (as required by the schedule-usually three) that are entered as one unit in a judged show.

CONDITION: The cultural appearance of horticulture exhibits at the time of judging.

COROLLA: The unit formed by the lobes (petals) of a blossom. The lobes may be separate or united as in the case of African violet blossoms.

CROWN: The head of the plant above the soil line. African violets are described as having single or multiple crowns

CULTIVAR: A horticulturally derived variety of a plant, as distinguished from a natural variety. Through common usage, the words "cultivar" and "variety" are interchangeable.

DISBUD: To remove buds for the purpose of encouraging maximum growth and timing of floriferousness of plants for exhibition.

DOUBLE POTTING: The placement of a plant, still in its smaller pot, within a larger pot with the space between the two pots filled with soil mix. This extension of the pot's diameter provides leaf support and is the equivalent of a flared top pot. Double potting is not permitted in AVSA shows.

DRENCH: To wet thoroughly; saturate.

ENTRY: A plant or other unit of a competitive show before it has been processed by the show committee and placed in a specific class.

EXHIBIT: An exhibit is an entry *after* it has been processed and placed in a class.

FAMILY: A taxonomic group (and nomenclatural category) comprised of one or more genera having certain basic characteristics in common.

Genus (plural, *genera):* The subdivision of a family. *Saintpaulia* is a genus of the family Gesneriaceae. Among others in the gesneriad family are *Achimenes, Aescananthus, Columnea, Episcia, Nematanthus, Sinningia, Smithiantha, Streptocarpus.*

Species: A subdivision of a genus. *Saintpaulia ionantha (S. ionantha)* is a species of the genus *Saintpaulia.* The new taxonomy (2006) lists six species: *S. goetzeana, S. inconspicua, S. ionantha, S. pusilla, S. shumensis, and S. teitensis.*

Subspecies: A subdivision of a species. Subspecies have differences between each other, but they are not considered unique enough to stand alone as separate species. The 2006 taxonomic reclassification created these subspecies for genus *Saintpaulia* species *ionantha*: grandifolia, grotei, ionantha, mafiensis, nitida, occidentalis, orbicularis, pendula, rupicola, and velutina.

Variety: A subdivision of a species or subspecies. A plant similar to the species under which it is classified but not different enough to be classified separately. The 2006 taxonomic reclassification created two varieties under subspecies ionantha. These are variety diplotricha and variety ionantha.

FERTILIZER: A soil enriching material comprised of one or more of the thirteen elements required for proper plant growth.

FLARED-TOP POT: A pot designed with an extended lip that serves as an additional support to the foliage. This type of pot is not permitted in an AVSA show.

FLORIFEROUSNESS (flor-if-er-ous-ness): The quantity of bloom on a plant.

FOLIAGE: The leaves of a plant collectively.

FOLIAGE TYPES: Foliage type is another means by which African violets are classified for competitive showing. The *AVML* and *First Class* give the official foliage description of the varieties. This description is usually furnished by the hybridizer. There are many shapes and textures of African violet foliage/leaves. (See Learn the Language – Foliage Types, p. 12.)

HUMIDITY/RELATIVE HUMIDITY: The ratio, expressed as a percentage, of the amount of water vapor actually in the air to the total amount present during saturation at the same temperature.

HYBRID: A plant grown from seed as a result of breeding or cross-pollinating different cultivars or species.

HYBRIDIZER: One who breeds or cross-pollinates plants.

LOBE (or petal): One of the divisions or leaf-like parts of a corolla. Lobe is the preferred term for gesneriad blossoms.

LEACH: To pour a quantity of plain water through the soil of a plant to flush away accumulated fertilizer salts and neutralize alkali build-up.

LEAF CUTTING: A leaf, plus usually a portion of the petiole, cut from a plant and used for propagating purposes. Sometimes referred to as the "mother" leaf.

LEAF TYPES: See FOLIAGE TYPES.

MATTING: Any synthetic material (carpeting, blanket, fleece, felt) that is used for lining the bottom of a tray for capillary mat watering.

Mother leaf: See LEAF CUTTING.

MUTATION: A plant that shows a marked change from the parent stock. This may be a natural mutation or the result of an application of a chemical or irradiation. See SPORT.

PASTEURIZE: To raise the temperature of the soil or potting mix (or one of the components) to 180°F and maintain that temperature for 30 minutes. This process kills undesirable pests and pathogens but does not destroy beneficial microorganisms.

PATHOGEN: Any agent that causes disease; a virus or a microorganism such as a bacterium or fungus.

PEAT MOSS: A light brown, fiberous, organic material formed partially or wholly from sphagnum mosses in a decomposed state and mined from bogs.

PEDICEL: The stem emanating from the peduncle and supporting the individual blossom in a flower cluster.

PEDUNCLE: The stem emanating from an axil and supporting the entire flower cluster.

PERLITE: Lightweight, porous, gritty, white pebbly material manufactured from crushed lava rock expanded to many times its original size through intense heat.

PETIOLE: The stem emanating from the main stem of the plant and supporting the leaf.

pH (Puissance de Hydrogen): The expression of the relative level of acidity or alkalinity of any substance. 7.0 is neutral, above 7.0 is alkaline and below 7.0 is acidic.

PLANTLET: An immature plant attached to the "mother" leaf or potted individually. See STARTER PLANTS.

PLANT TYPES: The following types of African violets are recognized by AVSA and are being bred by hybridizers specifically as one type or another: single-crowned standards, miniatures, semiminiatures, trailers and species. (See Learn the Language, p. 9.)

PROPAGATE: To produce, or cause to produce, new plants.

ROOTED CLUMP: A term used by commercial growers to refer to a group of plantlets attached to the leaf cutting ("mother" leaf).

ROSETTE: A cluster of leaves radiating symmetrically from a central stem. In reference to awards, a ribbon decoration gathered or pleated in a circular pattern and usually with one or more streamers attached.

SEEDLING: A plant grown from seed. After the plant has been propagated vegetatively from a leaf cutting, the resulting plants are no longer regarded as seedlings.

Species: See FAMILY

SPHAGNUM MOSS: A long-fibered moss in a less decomposed state than that of sphagnum peat moss. It is often used in its natural, unmilled state as a growing medium for plants such as bromeliads.

SPORT: A plant that shows a marked change from the parent plant. See MUTATION.

STARTER PLANTS: A term used by commercial growers to refer to immature plants in small (usually 2-1/2") pots.

STEM: The main stalk or trunk of a plant.

SUCKER: The beginning of a new plant which forms near the base of a plant or in the lower axils. For judging purposes in an African violet show, a sucker is not counted as such unless it shows four leaves and no sign of a bud. A sucker on a single-crowned specimen plant disqualifies it from being entered in a show since the plant is no longer considered to have a single crown.

SYSTEMIC: A chemical substance, which, when absorbed by plant tissue, causes the tissue to be poisonous to certain pests and diseases.

SYMMETRY: The degree of a perfect circular pattern of foliage; overlapping of foliage evenly spaced around the main stem of the plant; straight petioles with each layer of leaves progressively larger than the preceding layer.

TAXONOMY: A subsection of Biology concerned with the placement of organisms into categories within a classification system.

TISSUE CULTURE (inflorescent culture): Test tube propagation using a culture medium and producing hundreds of plants from a minute piece of plant tissue.

Trailer: See PLANT TYPES

VERMICULITE: A sterile, lightweight, brownish, soft-textured, pebbly material. It is manufactured from crushed mica ore expanded to many times its original size through intense heat.

VARIETY: Through common usage, the terms "cultivar" and "variety" have the same meaning.

Variegated Foliage: See FOLIAGE TYPES.

WETTING AGENT: A solution that is mixed with water to reduce the surface tension that causes water to bead.

WICKING: Any synthetic material used to draw water from a reservoir into the soil of a potted plant.